✳ new york's
50 best
places to
take tea

By Bo Niles

universe publishing

For Helene Silver, dear friend and creator of City & Company and the 50 Best Series, and for Jane Magidson, Emily Scharf, and Cindy Krause. With love and thanks for sharing afternoons over endless cups of tea.

First published in the United States of America in 2008 by
Universe Publishing
A Division of Rizzoli International Publications, Inc.
300 Park Avenue South
New York, NY 10010
www.rizzoliusa.com

© 2007 by Bo Niles

2008 2009 2010 2011 / 10 9 8 7 6 5 4 3 2 1

Designed by Headcase Design
Printed in the United States of America

ISBN-13: 978-0-7893-1586-1
ISBN-10: 0-7893-1586-6
Library of Congress Catalog Control Number: 2007936981

PUBLISHER'S NOTE

Neither Universe nor the author has any interest, financial or personal, in the establishments listed in this book. No fees were paid or services rendered in exchange for inclusion in these pages. While every effort was made to ensure accuracy at the time of publication, it is always best to call ahead and confirm that the information is up-to-date.

contents

AND SOME MORE!

GLOSSARY AND INDEX

a civilized sip

Taking tea is a convivial activity, a perfect way for friends, loved ones, and even business associates to get together—and it is an equally lovely and salutary way to enjoy a solitary, even soulful, interlude during a busy day.

Why tea?

Tea is both elixir and tonic. Tea is timeless.

So utterly of the moment when you sip it, tea is the one beverage that also gently invokes the past...while conjuring up the future in its leaves. At once stimulating and soothing, tea rejuvenates and relaxes the body and soul. No other drink can make the same claim.

Time was when many tea venues around town offered only a handful of teas. As taking tea has surged in popularity, some tearooms have increased their inventories; some even into the hundreds. In Manhattan, you will find a tea for every taste, from bracing Assams to decorous Darjeelings to zippy, tapioca-studded "bubble" teas. Like New York and New Yorkers, tea is marvelously diverse.

In this fourth edition of what used to be entitled *The New York Book of Tea*, I have whittled the choice of tea venues down to those I feel are the fifty best that Manhattan has to offer. Many predicate their offerings on the British standard of a three-course afternoon tea. A number of teas, notably those presented by some of the city's most luxurious hotels, are resplendent prix fixe repasts. Teas taken in more informal venues are more relaxed, with myriad offerings to order à la carte. In every case, it is advisable to call ahead to see if it is necessary to reserve—and to double-check prices, because these change more often than one might expect.

Enjoy!

the legendary origins of tea

Tea, it is said, was discovered in China in the third millennium B.C. by Emperor Shen Nong. Attentive to matters of health and hygiene, the emperor was fastidious in such practices as boiling water. On one occasion, as he stoked the fire under his kettle, he plucked branches from a shrub close at hand and tossed them into the flames. A few leaves floated, by accident, into the water. As the leaves colored the liquid, the emperor, marveling at the fragrance that arose from the kettle, sipped the brew. Captivated by its flavor, and by the stimulating feelings it engendered, he hastened to advocate ch'a—or tea—as an antidote for a plethora of ills ranging from indigestion to lethargy.

Almost ten centuries later, in his renowned *Book of Tea*, the venerated Chinese poet Lu Yu described how the ritual of preparing and presenting tea—what came to be known as the tea ceremony—mirrored an inward ethic that embraced respect and courtesy. Within this simple, generous—and beautiful—act of brewing and pouring tea, a harmony between host and guest could be realized, a harmony underlying all of life. Tea was—and is—a work of art.

the health benefits of tea

Much has been written about how tea—especially green tea—reduces blood pressure, helps prevent liver and heart disease, lowers cholesterol, and aids and improves digestion. Green tea has also been cited as possibly averting stroke and a number of cancers, including cancers of the skin, colon, stomach, esophagus, breast, and prostate. Because tea contains fluoride, it is also said to fight the bacteria responsible for tooth decay and gingivitis. Some claim that tea also strengthens bones.

Tea is considered so healthy because it contains polyphenols and flavenoids, which are naturally occurring compounds that act as antioxidants to ward off cancer-causing free radicals. White and green teas contain the highest portion of these beneficial attributes.

Tea is a short-term stimulant, and usually does not cause heightened nervousness or insomnia, like coffee; nor does it irritate the stomach. This is because the caffeine in tea is water-soluble, so it passes through the digestive system more quickly than the insoluble caffeine in coffee.

Some herbal teas, notably chamomile and peppermint, are sipped to aid digestion and minimize bloating and flatulence. Dieters turn to chicory tea to curb their appetites, and to berry teas to lower cholesterol. Insomniacs often find that a lavender-infused tea soothes them into slumber.

Despite their claims, some herbal teas may induce an allergic reaction. Nutritionists recommend that you try a new herbal tea in a very small dose—less than half a cup, at most—to make sure you do not incur an adverse reaction to the flower, herb, or root that flavors that particular tea.

Even if you do not ingest tea strictly for your health, you can still derive superficial health benefits from it. Chilled, dampened tea bags, for example, are an antidote to sunburn, cooling the skin while tannins stanch the sting. Cool, moist tea bags may also reduce puffiness around the eyes—a good trick to try after a night on the town.

the british tradition of afternoon tea

Afternoon tea in Britain—like Christmas trees and Santa Claus—is a "tradition" that was invented by the Victorians. Unlike high tea, the robust meal the British working classes returned to after a long day laboring at the factory, afternoon tea was a formal, aristocratic affectation that evolved as a genteel ritual to punctuate the long interval between luncheon and evening supper.

The proper afternoon tea encountered today in New York consists, in the main, of the traditional three courses, which may be served simultaneously on a tiered cake stand or as a sequence of separate plates. The presentation of a full afternoon tea menu allows you to graze at your leisure. Most tea takers typically, and sensibly, follow the menu in the traditional manner, first nibbling on finger sandwiches and other savories, then on scones or crumpets accompanied by clotted cream and preserves, and finally sampling a medley of sweets, from simple cakes to delicate crèmes brulées.

In a formal set-up, tea is usually of the loose-leaf variety, although many venues—even some posh hotels—rely on tea bags. The finest service presents brewing tea and hot water in matching pots, perhaps with a tea cozy to maintain their warmth. Hot water should be replenished at least once during your tea; if not, you should be able to request it.

The first course typically comprises a medley of finger sandwiches made from white, whole-wheat, or pumpernickel bread, cut into bite-sized, crustless geometric shapes. Fillings often include peeled, sliced cucumber, de-stemmed watercress, egg salad, sliced white chicken, salmon, miniature shrimp, or rare beef. Some menus dazzle with inventive fillings or relishes to spice up the basics.

The second course is usually a scone or two accompanied by Devonshire cream—a thick whipped or clotted cream—plus a choice of preserves and marmalade. The third sweet course adds miniature petits fours, éclairs, tartlets filled with lemon curd or berries in custard, and perhaps a cookie or two. Some venues add fresh fruit or nuts. Another festive extra, at an additional charge, is a glass of champagne or sparkling wine, sherry, or port.

tea ceremonies

The Japanese Tea Ceremony

The meditative practice known as the tea ceremony honors a series of rituals. The *sukiya*, or teahouse, and its components—the *midsuya*, an anteroom where utensils are collected and prepared; the *machiai*, or porch where guests gather and await their host; and the *roji*, a garden path guests must traverse as they approach the teahouse itself—express the Zen ideal of austere and humble rusticity.

In preparation to enter the tearoom, guests remove their shoes, then sit and wait to be summoned across a pathway. The path is traditionally composed of moistened stones set in an irregular manner, which forces guests to slow down and focus their attention on the ceremony to come. To purify themselves, guests wash their hands and mouth at the *tsukubai*, a stone basin filled with fresh water. They then pass through a gate that symbolizes their exit from the world outside into the world of the tearoom. The doorway into the tearoom itself is only three feet high; everyone must stoop to enter.

The tearoom, or *chashitsu*, is empty save for tatami mats that cover the floor and a small square sunken hearth called the *ro*, which contains the *kuro*, a tiny stove used to heat the *kama*, or kettle. (During warmer months, a brazier may be used instead.) At one end of the room an elevated alcove called the *tokonoma* typically exhibits a scroll, or *kakemono*, brushed with calligraphy expressing the theme of the ceremony, plus a simple flower arrangement meant to symbolize the fleeting beauty of nature. These are to be contemplated by the guests as they take their places.

Much of the tea ceremony consists of cleansing and purifying the utensils so that they can be contemplated and appreciated for their rustic beauty. The serving of tea is a cleansing experience, too, as every gesture, from the bow of thanks when offered the cup to the bow of thanks when the cup is passed from one guest to the next, is purged of gratuitous flourishes.

Pure mineral water for the tea is held in a special jar only the host may touch called a *mizushashi*. Powdered green *matcha* is stored in a *chaire*, a ceramic container kept in a silk pouch. There are a number of ritualized steps in the preparation of the tea, but eventually, with a bamboo ladle called a *hishaku*, the hot water from the kama is poured over the matcha (which has been measured into a bowl called a *chawan*); the two are whisked into a thin paste with a bamboo whisk called a *chasen*. More water is then added, and the tea whisked once again to create a foam on top. The chawan passes from host to the main guest, and thence from guest to guest, as the presentation is discussed amongst all. A second, thinner tea is prepared and poured into individual cups and sweets are served before the ceremony comes to a close.

The Chinese Gongfu Tea Ceremony

Like the Japanese tea ceremony, the Chinese method of brewing and serving tea—called *Gongfu*—is a serene ritual wherein one calms and stills one's soul.

The Chinese revere teapots known as *Yixing*. Large enough only to hold a few mouthfuls of tea, these teapots are handcrafted of a fine, porous clay that absorbs the flavor of the tea leaves. When new, the teapot must be 'cured' by boiling tea leaves in it so that the flavor can enter the pores of the clay.

At the outset of the tea presentation, all vessels are rinsed with hot water, which symbolically purifies them for the ceremony. After rinsing, tea leaves are measured into the teapot—usually about two teaspoons—and the pot is set into a large bowl called a chawan. Hot but not boiling water is poured into the teapot until it overflows, and the excess water runs down the sides into the bowl. The overflow insures that no bubbles remain in the pot to roil the tea and that the tea is hot all the way through. Oolong and black teas are typically steeped for about three minutes.

The tea undergoes three pours: from the teapot into a serving pitcher; from the pitcher into a *wen xiang bei*, or aroma cup; and from the aroma cup into the *cha bei*, or drinking cup. When the aroma cup has been emptied, it is lifted to the nose so that the fragrance of the tea may be appreciated. The proper way to drink a cup is to take two to four swallows. During the presentation, the brewing process is repeated two or three more times. Each successive steeping takes a little longer to extract the flavor of the tea leaves. Between each steeping, the water must be reheated to the correct temperature—but never to a boil.

The Chinese Gaiwan Tea Ceremony

In this version of the tea ceremony, tea is brewed in a small, lidded bowl called a *gaiwan*. After the ritual rinsing, one or two teaspoons of tea leaves are measured into the gaiwan. A few drops of hot water are sprinkled over the tea leaves to release their scent, which is inhaled and appreciated. The initial sprinkling also allows tightly wound or balled tea leaves to begin to unfurl. Hot water is poured over the leaves, and once the lid has been replaced, the tea is allowed to steep, usually for about three minutes. The lidded bowl and the saucer on which it rests are then lifted in one hand. The lid is slightly tilted to allow the tea to be poured into the drinking cup while holding back the leaves.

The Korean Tea Ceremony

In Korea, *Dah-do*—Tea Tao, or the way of tea—is a meditative act evocative of the Zen approach to tea, which quietly exhorts those present to be in harmony with nature, to feel removed from the outside world, and to be elegant and graceful in the presentation of the tea.

The tea set, called a *dagi*, consists of a teapot (*chuchonja*), teacups (*chat chans*), coasters, a scoop, a small lipped bowl called a *sookwu* for serving the tea, a large bowl for discarded water, a tea towel (*chat sukon*), and a mat called a dapo.

Utensils that do not touch water—the canister, coasters, and the scoop—are placed on the mat. The chuchonja and chat chans are rinsed with hot water and, separately, hot water is poured into the lipped sookwu. Tea leaves—about one teaspoon per person—are measured into the chuchonja, and the now slightly cooled water in the sookwu is poured over them. The chuchonja is swirled three times and the water discarded. The sookwu is then refilled with hot water at the correct temperature, which is poured into the chuchonja, and swirled three times once again.

The rinse water is poured out of the teacups, and the tea is poured. Each cup is filled only a third of the way, then to two-thirds, then to the rim; this rotation of the pouring insures that the tea is consistent from one cup to another. Once the chat chans are full, a coaster is placed under each; they are then slid across the table to the guests. A prayer is said, after which everyone bows; the fragrance of the tea is admired; and everyone drinks. Tea can be infused two or three more times; each successive brew takes somewhat longer than the last.

using this book

Venues are listed alphabetically in the Table of Contents; to identify a venue by neighborhood, please turn to the Index by Neighborhood at the back of the book.

Price ranges are indicated by the "$" symbol. A single symbol refers to inexpensive menus, which are largely à la carte. Two symbols signify moderately priced teas; these describe either à la carte or set menus. Three symbols reflect the most costly teas, which tend to be those offered by hotels noted for their elegant venues and styles of presentation.

Translated roughly into sum, "$" teas cost under $15; "$$" teas range from about $15 to $30; and "$$$" teas run from $30 to $45 and up.

Please note that most hotels require a reservation for afternoon tea, as do some of the tearooms. To be certain you will be accommodated at the time you desire, it is advisable to telephone ahead. It is wise to check on prices then, too, as they can increase from time to time.

*new york's
50 best
places to
take tea

alice's tea cup

102 West 73rd Street
bet. Columbus and Amsterdam Avenues
212-799-3006
www.alicesteacup.com
Hours: Daily "before and after noon"
Price Range: $$

On the Upper West Side, Alice's Tea Cup, named after the plucky heroine who slipped *Through the Looking Glass*, has become an institution. The tearoom—two rooms actually—is a cozy spot to hang out over a cup of tea (there are a hundred to choose from) and a crumble-on-your-bib scone or sweet. Roomy tables provide ample space to spread out and browse a book or newspaper if sipping solo.

Owners Lauren and Haley Fox and Michael Eisenberg offer three prix fixe afternoon teas, each more abundant than the last, as well as a Wee Tea for children under the age of ten. The Nibble consists of a fat pot of tea served with a little sponge under the spout to catch drips, a choice of scone with preserves and whipped cream, a choice of sandwich, and cookies. The Mad Hatter includes a three-cup pot of tea and scone, plus a choice of Chai Crème Brûlée or Jean's Not-Yet-but-Soon-to-be-Famous Mocha Chocolate Chip Cake. The Jabberwocky gives you...everything!

The children's Wee Tea includes an herbal or fruit tea and scone, plus a serving of the White Rabbit Dark Chocolate Mousse with Milk Chocolate Shavings—which can also be enjoyed à la carte by suitably appreciative grown-ups.

For Upper East Siders, Alice's Tea Cup recently opened a pair of outposts north of Bloomingdale's, one on East 64th Street and the other on East 81st Street. Called Alice's Tea Cup Chapters II and III, these locations more or less clone their sister's West Side ambience. In all three locations, waitresses wear the obligatory fairy-tale wings and glitter.

All is as it should be in Wonderland.

american girl café

AT AMERICAN GIRL PLACE

609 Fifth Avenue
Entrance on East 49th Street
bet. Fifth and Madison Avenues
1-877-AG-PLACE
(1-877-247-5223)
www.americangirl.com
Hours: Daily, 4 P.M.; reserved seating only
Price Range: $$

Never underestimate the power of a woman—or a little girl. More than twenty years ago, the first American Girl historical-character dolls made their debut; since then, the brand has sold more than 105 million books and millions of dolls.

Developing three emporia—in Chicago, New York, and Los Angeles—was the next logical step. Conveniently situated across the street from Saks, the Manhattan venue is not merely a shop—it is an entertainment complex where a little girl and her family and friends can book an entire day to partake of the American Girl experience. This includes a viewing of The American Girls Musical Revue at the in-house theater, a CD, spending money, a souvenir doll T-shirt, and a meal—which can be afternoon tea.

The café—an exuberant candy-box of a room featuring black-and-white striped walls, daisy-splashed banquettes, and jewel-fringed lampshades—is without a doubt the most gleeful of all the city's tearooms. It is also surprisingly sophisticated, with a jazz track that purrs in the background and a "big city" aura that will make any girl feel special. Everything here is calculated to charm, from Treat Seats for dolls so they won't miss out on any of the fun, to fanciful polka-dotted Table Talker boxes filled with queries to "get conversations going." One card posed a very adult question: "Have you ever been told you couldn't do something because you're female?" There are even loaner dolls for little (and big) girls who left theirs at home.

The prix fixe tea opens with a Warm Welcome of cinnamon buns, then proceeds to entrées and Sweet Surprises named for various American Place dolls—plus a specialty mini Chocolate Mousse Flowerpot.

arium

31 Little West 12th Street
bet. Ninth Avenue and Washington Street
212-463-8630
www.ariumnyc.com
Hours: Tuesday through Sunday 3 P.M. to 6 P.M.
Price Range: $$

The brainchild of entrepreneur and self-proclaimed "arts philanthropist" Philip Pelusi, Arium—which bends the Latin a bit to mean "meeting place"—is like Mr. Pelusi himself: multi-faceted. Yes, Arium is a tea room, but it is also a café, gallery, and wine bar. In other words, a place to have brunch, enjoy a drink, listen to jazz or a classical concert (on its own grand piano), enjoy an art exhibit, or attend a (free) film screening. Arium also hosts corporate events and private parties.

Due to Pelusi's fame as a hair stylist (he trademarked the so-called Volumetrics haircutting technique), Arium neighbors one of Pelusi's beauty salons (he owns fourteen). So, as you are conversing with your companion over a cup of Buddha's Finger oolong or ultra-rare Chinese Yellow, your words may well be underscored by the gentle hum of a hair dryer next door.

Arium prides itself on offering more than 100 teas in virtually every imaginable scent and hue. The airy restaurant-cum-gallery, which overlooks cobble-stoned West 12th Street, is dotted with tables draped in damask that are sensibly protected by glass. Tablewares are pretty, gilt-edged, and English, all accented with flowers. (Even the bar displays tea things in lieu of the standard line-up of bottles.)

At tea time, you are presented with four menu options. Light Tea includes a pot of tea plus one of three courses; Middle Tea offers two courses; Grand Tea, three; and the Royal Tea adds a flute of Champagne. The choice of courses is up to you. For a single, you may opt for the first course, composed of scones and accompaniments; or the second course, which assembles mini savories such as smoked duck pate on crostini or a mini spinach quiche; or the third, which boasts four sweets, including a chocolate raspberry torte.

the astor court

AT THE SAINT REGIS HOTEL

2 East 55th Street
bet. Fifth and Madison Avenues
212-339-6857
www.stregis.com
Hours: Daily 3:15 P.M. to 5:15 P.M.
Price Range: $$$

Raised on a pretty balustraded dais just inside one of the front doors to the St. Regis (look for the one that's closer to Madison Avenue), the Astor Court appears to be suspended under a timeless, cloud-frothed sky. Encircling the room is a mural painted by artist Zhou Sha Liang, which depicts the "Greek ideals of peace, harmony, and beauty." Brushed in pale pastels, the mural is as confectionary in spirit as the traditional three-course tea served every afternoon.

The Astor Court's dozen or so tables, each ringed by celadon velvet-upholstered armchairs of a Louis XVI persuasion, cluster around a central pedestal bearing an enormous arrangement of seasonal blooms. An immense chandelier casts a soft light overhead. Table settings feature linens from Porthault and porcelain from Limoges by way of Tiffany & Company, all exclusive to the hotel. Individual tea strainers and small bud vases complete the harmonious scheme, as do rock-sugar sticks to sweeten your brew, which is served in a silver-plated tea pot.

The St. Regis claims that its prix fixe tea "links the solemnity of the Japanese tea ceremony and sustaining high tea of British schoolchildren." Indeed, taking tea is a delicious education here, with every one of the hotel's two dozen teas elucidated in a book, along with precise information about how each is brewed. Special teas to note are the hotel's five unique blends, which include Yellow and Blue, a Floral Rapture, and a specially selected tea of the week.

If, after tea, you feel like something alcoholic, you can repair to the adjoining King Cole Bar with its glorious mural by Maxfield Parrish of the slightly dyspeptic Royal. Your cue to make your move? When strains of the teatime harp segue into the soft tones of a barroom piano.

bar seine

AT THE PLAZA ATHENÉE HOTEL

37 East 64th Street
bet. Madison and Park Avenues
212-734-9100
www.arabellerestaurant.com
Hours: Daily 2:30 P.M. to 5 P.M.
Price Range: $$$

Curved red awnings and a matching canopy usher guests into the Plaza Athenée (and its companion restaurant, Arabelle) with Parisian panache. At the rear of the airy lobby, leafy murals frame the elevator bank and, to its immediate left, an arched glass entrance leads into the intimate rooms comprising the Bar Seine, where drinks—and high tea—are served each afternoon.

These cozy rooms are softly lit by sconces fronted by translucent discs of alabaster-like stone, and by lamps set behind each of the eleven tables located within. Heavy velvet draperies separate two of the spaces; the third contains the bar. In all three, leather-toned walls present a handsome backdrop for a collection of paintings; sumptuous banquettes clad in leather or velvet; tufted armchairs; bamboo side chairs that can be moved at will to suit the size of the party; and commodious tables in a walnut hue that matches the floor.

The Plaza Athenée's high tea, prepared in Arabelle's kitchens, is offered both à la carte and as a prix fixe three-course affair. If there are just two of you, you might prefer to order one full tea plus an extra pot for your companion. Miniature tea sandwiches, two fresh-baked scones, petite pastries, and a truffle or two arrive on a triple-tiered stand; clotted cream, jams and preserves, rock-sugar sticks, and cream are set out on a separate tray.

Bar Seine offers a total of fifteen teas, including a Plaza Athenée Luxury Blend that combines Darjeeling, China Rose, and Earl Grey teas, and a Jet Lag Herbal Blend with the subtle scent of anise, as well as assorted Twinings' teas.

bette

461 West 23rd Street
bet. Ninth and Tenth Avenues
212-366-0404
www.betterestaurant.com
Hours: Private parties, as reserved
Price Range: $$$$

Bette, at the Tenth Avenue corner of the London Terrace apartment block on West 23rd Street, is situated mere steps from the bustling West Chelsea art scene. The restaurant-cum-tearoom—designed by Diana Vignoly with architect Christina Buzzetti— is also something of a mission for owner Amy Sacco (who also owns Lot 61 and Bungalow 8). As co-founder of Art Production Fund, a non-profit that helps artists "realize difficult-to-produce works," Sacco created Bette to showcase site-specific works by artists such as Damian Hirst and Jeremy Blake. Here, the highlight is an enormous tapestry by artist Richard Phillips that features striking images of four gorgeous women—the "Bettes."

Sunlight pours through arched windows at the front of the room onto walnut wainscoting and soft-hued stucco walls. Huge floral arrangements on the windowsill cast shadows across the ebonized floor. A stylish 1930s sofa topped with gold-tinted glass separates the dining area from the bar, while upholstered armless chairs shrug their pert shoulders like svelte models in strapless gowns. To mute the sounds of conversation, the ceiling is carpeted in striated sage broadloom patterned with vines. Rubberized mats cover tabletops; settings mix fine china with orchid-filled vases.

Although Bette no longer does walk-in teas for afternoon strollers in the neighborhood, they are pleased to offer a unique luxurious experience for private parties. As with any special event, such as a shower, the menu is tailored to your group and must be arranged ahead of time. Bette's specially blended teas include two rare and delicate whites. Traditional accompaniments are prepared with exquisite attention by chef Ken Addington; these typically include some delicious surprises, such as passionflower curd instead of the usual lemon.

bg

AT BERGDORF GOODMAN

754 Fifth Avenue
bet. 57th and 58th Streets
212-872-8977
www.bergdorfgoodman.com
Hours: Monday through Friday 3 P.M. to 5 P.M.
Price Range: $$$

Bergdorf's has long dedicated its seventh floor to beautiful things relating to the home, from linens for the bed to tableware. So, it makes perfect sense for them to have created a restaurant here that functions as a gathering place for shoppers, tourists, and New Yorkers looking for a quiet retreat where they can conduct business or meet with friends—or gossip at one of the tables flanked by "whispering chairs," which mute tête-à-têtes. (If you desire one of these tables, ask for nos. 1 or 2, which look directly over the park.)

The enfilade of rooms that make up the restaurant —and its bar—are inspired by the tenth-floor apartment "with its million-dollar view," once occupied by the Goodmans. The paneling in the bar presumably mimics that in Mr. Goodman's office/library; the space adjoining it has walls sheathed in pale blue hand-painted French silk, as per the Goodman's dining room. The farthest room is paneled, too, but here its geometric shapes are mirrored and outlined in black, gold, and a chic chartreuse that adds an extra punch to all the non-paneled surfaces as well.

Mirrors refract the light and the view, and shimmer like jewels as the three-course prix fixe afternoon tea arrives. The palette of teas ranges from Marco Polo, a subtly perfumed black, to spicy Chandernagor, a liquor-infused Bourbon, and Eros, which mingles hibiscus and "mauve flowers." A separate menu of desserts by pâtissier Sergio Sosa is available to round things off, and you can add a flute of Veuve Clicquot to upgrade the service to a Tea Royale.

café sabarsky

AT THE NEUE GALERIE

1048 Fifth Avenue
at 86th Street
212-288-0665
www.neuegalerie.org
Hours: Monday and Wednesday 9 A.M. to
6 P.M.; Thursday through Sunday 9 A.M. to
9 P.M.; closed Tuesday; (open Wednesday
and Thursday when museum is closed).
Price Range: $$

Rarely does a new museum open in New York, so it's no surprise that lines form outside this mansion-museum dedicated to early twentieth-century German and Austrian art and design. Conceived and bankrolled by the former U.S. Ambassador to Austria and art collector Ronald S. Lauder, the Neue Galerie, once the home of Mrs. Cornelius Vanderbilt III, has been impeccably restored inside and out.

Not the least of the museum's pleasures is Café Sabarsky (named for museum co-founder and art dealer Serge Sabarsky, a friend of Lauder's who died in 1995), an elegant, wood-paneled recreation of a turn-of-the-century Viennese café on the ground level of the museum. Lines form here, too, and no wonder: rich and evocative details abound. Banquettes are upholstered in rose-dappled acid-green velveteen in a 1912 pattern by Otto Wagner; the café tables are encircled by bentwood chairs after an 1899 design by Adolf Loos; and lighting fixtures are period Josef Hoffman designs. A fireplace and an enormous, seasonal floral arrangement dominate one end of the room.

Although the café offers delicacies specific to every meal, it holds particular appeal at teatime, when a pot of Ceylon or chamomile-lavender or pineapple-papaya tea (or a *caffe mit schlag*) perfectly offsets a patisserie created by chef Kurt Gutenbrunner. Tea is presented in the Viennese manner, on a little oval metal tray in a very striking glass teapot. Try the Mandel Meringue, or the strudel, or—so quintessentially Viennese—the Linzertorte.

In the basement, the Neue Galerie's snappy, all black-and-white Café Fledermaus handles overflow crowds and serves as a venue for special events such as film screenings.

café sfa

AT SAKS FIFTH AVENUE

611 Fifth Avenue
bet. 49th and 50th Streets
212-753-4000
www.saksfifthavenue.com
Hours: Monday through Friday 3 P.M. to 5 P.M.
Price Range: $$

What fate could be worse than to collapse from hunger midway through a shopping spree along Fifth Avenue? To counter such a threat, Saks created a casual yet elegant eighth-floor café that offers a proper afternoon tea. Here, walls striated in a warm shade of cognac are offset by floors swathed in crumb-camouflaging tweed, creating the perfect environment to enjoy a prix fixe or à la carte tea, whether you are alone or with a shopping buddy.

Because the room tends to be less crowded at teatime, you should find a seat easily at one of the tables perched on the loggia level along the perimeter of the café, looking out at one of two iconic Manhattan views: the twin spires of St. Patrick's Cathedral or the most beautiful complex in the city, Rockefeller Center, and a bird's eye look at the intimate landscaped lawn on top of the center's lower building to the north of the promenade. From this vantage point, during the winter, you can also catch a glimpse of an agile skater performing a double-axel on the Rocke-feller Plaza ice rink.

As you unwind, your tea arrives on the traditional tiered stand: assorted sandwiches, homemade scones and muffins with lemon curd, Devonshire cream and 'spoon' fruit jams, gourmet cookies, and mini chocolate truffles.

Teas, provided by San Francisco-based tea store Mighty Leaf, come in a dozen flavors, including Breakfast Americana and Celebration, a Chinese black infused with Guyanese fruit, which should propel you to your feet and back to Saks' fashion floors with renewed vigor.

If you are mad for sweets, Saks has located its chic, modernist Charbonnnel et Walker Chocolate Café on this same floor, so you can stop by for a chocolate fix on your way back to the escalator.

café 2 and terrace 5

AT THE MUSEUM OF MODERN ART

611 West 53rd Street
bet. Fifth and Sixth Avenues
212-708-9400
www.MoMA.org
Hours: Daily 11 A.M. to 5 P.M.; Friday 11
   A.M. to 7:30 P.M. (closed Tuesdays)
Price Range: $

As a self-confessed aficionado of minimalist art and architecture, I always feel perfectly at home at the new Museum of Modern Art, designed by Japanese architect Yoshio Taniguchi—especially when enjoying a cup of tea and a sweet in either of MoMA's welcoming, casual cafés. Whenever I go to the museum, I make a point of stopping for a spell just to enjoy the atmosphere of the place after viewing a special exhibition or revisiting some of my favorite works of art.

Café 2 is the more convivial of the two venues and accommodates many more visitors (and has a more ample menu) in its refectory-style space with long communal tables. Café 2 also offers a quick pick-me-up at a separate espresso bar located at the entrance into the dining room. For an afternoon museum excursion, though, my preference for a sip and a nibble is Terrace 5, a more intimate alcove located near the entrance of the painting and sculpture galleries on the fifth floor. Also known as the Carroll and Milton Petrie Café, after its benefactors (who are also credited with the Metropolitan Museum's Petrie Court, see page 84), this bright, white airy space lines up its commodious tables and curvy Arne Jacobsen chairs to take full advantage of a lively view through sheet glass across the museum's sculpture garden to its glass-gridded education center, which is beautifully juxtaposed against a slice of city skyline that includes the palazzo-like University Club.

MoMA offers five teas. Three are old-timers—English Breakfast, Earl Grey, and Darjeeling—and two are lighter teas—a floral jasmine green and an herbal "harmony." Both cafés also excel at authentic light or dark hot chocolate; both are complemented with a fudgey brownie. Other sweets include biscotti, cookies, plum tart, and a ricotta cheese cake

cha an

230 East 9th Street
bet. Second and Third Avenues
212-228-8030
Hours: Monday through Thursday 2 P.M. to
   11 P.M.; Friday and Saturday Noon to
   Midnight; Sunday Noon to 10 P.M.
Price Range: $$

This sanctuary's location on the second floor of a narrow row house elevates the room above the hubbub of the street and instills an atmosphere of calm, which allows denizens of Cha An to feel fully centered in body and in spirit.

Like authentic Japanese teahouses, the room has a gently rustic aspect. Walnut-stained ceilings and woodwork mix beautifully with tea-saturated concrete floors and screens made of bamboo. Smooth river rocks, chunks of rough-hewn stone, and ikebana-style flower arrangements provide decorative accents, while Western-style tables and chairs ensure comfort for those unaccustomed to kneeling on traditional tatami mats. In one corner near the front window, though, steps lead up to a private tea room where guests can kneel as they engage in the quiet ritual of the tea ceremony. The tea ceremony, for parties of four or fewer, may be requested in half-hour sessions.

At the other end of the tea house, a counter stretches the width of the room in front of the kitchen, which is fully visible behind a matchstick valance. White ceramic canisters stand boldly on shelves above the pass-through; teas at Cha An can also be purchased by the ounce.

The notebook–style menu has a section of teas, which are also illustrated on a "world tea map." Cha An's teas can be enjoyed by the pot or as part of their prix fixe afternoon tea—with sandwiches, scones, and sweets—which is served until 7 p.m. Two dessert teas are also available. In addition, Cha An serves one green tea, Neguynyin (named after the bodhisattva of compassion), in the kung-fu style. Foods include ice creams and green-tea truffles.

the cocktail terrace

AT THE WALDORF-ASTORIA HOTEL

301 Park Avenue
bet. 49th and 50th Streets
212-872-7919
www.hilton.com
Hours: Wednesday through Sunday 3 P.M. to
5:15 P.M.
Price Range: $$$

Listed as an Historic Hotel of America by the National Trust for Historic Preservation, the Waldorf-Astoria Hotel sits proudly on a prime patch of Manhattan turf just south of Saint Bartholomew's Church and has for decades served as a monument to hospitality for presidents and proletariat alike.

The prix fixe tea service at the Waldorf is offered on the spacious, two-story-high Cocktail Terrace just inside the Park Avenue entrance to the lobby. Elevated on a balcony accented with gilt railings, the terrace emulates the dining room of an Art Deco luxury liner. Islands of cushy seating—sink-into sofas clad in dusty-gold damask and comfy armchairs upholstered in rose and gold striped velvet—are well spaced on a luxuriant expanse of soft, conversation-muffling carpet. At the appropriate hour, every table is set with crisp white napery, elegant white china, and individual silver-plated tea strainers.

The Cocktail Terrace, which caters with equal aplomb to a young mother treating a trio of elementary-school girlfriends or a group of badge-wearing conventioneers, sensibly offers not one but three teas: Classic Afternoon Tea, with the usual triumvirate of nibbles (sandwiches, currant buttermilk scones with Devonshire cream and preserves, and "delicate" pastries); Light Tea, which eliminates the sandwiches; and Champagne Tea, which adds a "Classic Waldorf-Astoria Brut." Also sensible is the modest surcharge for anyone sharing another's tea.

For those who wish to linger for drinks, the bar on the terrace provides the perfect segue into the evening hours.

danal

90 East 10th Street
bet. Third and Fourth Avenues
212-982-6930
Hours: Friday and Saturday only, 4 P.M. to
6 P.M.; reservations required.
Price Range: $$$

Danal is tucked into a nondescript block on the fringes of the wholesale antiques district adjoining the East Village. Steps down from the street, the restaurant looks like a country inn transported to these shores intact from the English shires. A blue-tiled counter sets off the kitchen area at the front of the room. The dining area just behind is genially furnished with pine tables and mismatched chairs, scrubbed-pine dressers, and cupboards overflowing with crockery and teapots.

You can always order a pot of tea and a pastry alone or as part of a meal, but Danal's popular prix fixe afternoon tea, offered only on weekends, must be requested in advance by telephone. When you arrive, you are escorted upstairs to take your tea in the privacy of the restaurant's cheerful, second-level floor-through space. Here, bright yellow walls, a corner fireplace, Oriental rugs scattered higgledy-piggledy over the floor, and a huge front window bring warmth to the room.

Danal's selection of teas is extensive and embraces many varieties, including a lovely Chinese oolong, Goddess of Mercy, which is low in tannin and caffeine. Japanese sencha is poured warm, not hot, so that it can be properly savored. Several aromatics and fruit-flavored tisanes are also on the list, as well as three herbal infusions: chamomile, lemon verbena, and mint. Tea accompaniments are something of a surprise, as Danal relies on the chef's fancy—and yours—when preparing food for your personal delectation. Suffice it to say that Danal's afternoon tea always comprises a selection of wonderful tea sandwiches, fresh-baked scones, and desserts. Besides the intimacy of afternoon tea, Danal also caters tea parties for twelve to fifty people. These are particularly popular for bridal or baby showers.

the deco room at north square

AT THE WASHINGTON SQUARE HOTEL

103 Waverly Place
Northwest corner of Washington
Square Park at West 8th Street
212-254-1200
www.washingtonsquarehotel.com
www.northsquareny.com
Hours: Daily 3 P.M. to 5 P.M. (closed Sundays)
Price Range: $$

The dimly lit Deco Room-cum-bar, set discreetly behind a pair of wrought-iron gates at the rear of the Washington Square Hotel lobby, is the sort of lusciously moody spot that evokes the glamour of a luxury liner or train—in miniature. Matte black faux-pigskin banquettes line walls upholstered in soft, subtly-patterned mustard-hued velvet; these are offset by a coffered ceiling painted in a cubist manner in subtle earth tones. Small, curved armchairs with copper-toned seats pull up to octagonal tables, which stand about on the mosaic-tiled floors like small sculptures.

Tea for the Deco Room is prepared in the North Square Restaurant, which is located in the hotel but which can also be accessed directly from the street. Once you place your order, tea is brought to the table in a pot or in a two-cup press. Tea sandwiches, biscotti, and scones are presented in the traditional manner on a tiered stand. The Deco Room's eight teas, described picturesquely on the menu, hail from SerendipiTea, a purveyor of teas that subscribes to an environmentally responsible philosophy—all their teas are organically grown and plucked by hand.

Besides the old favorites, the line-up includes: Burrough's Brew, an organic black tea with a hint of coconut; ChocolaTea, which swirls essences of chocolate and vanilla into black tea blended with rooibos; Passion & Envy, a blend of Japanese sencha with passion fruit; and Ruby Sipper, an infusion that combines the essence of blood orange and pear. And for those dying for total release from a strenuous day, there's Zzz, which promotes the calming effects of lavender and chamomile.

franchia

12 Park Avenue
bet. 34th and 35th Streets
212-213-1001
www.franchia.com
Hours: Daily 3 P.M. to 5 P.M.
Price Range: $$

Dedicated to "reflecting harmony and balance in all things," Franchia—a self-styled "tea shrine in another space and time"—showcases its teas in a crisp, zen-like space entered through a neo-gothic doorway to the right of the canopy at the Ten Park Avenue Apartments. An offshoot of a beautiful nearby Korean restaurant called Hangawi, Franchia compartmentalizes its activities on three levels, which step up and back like terraces, affording glimpses from each to the next through hand-carved ebony rails. The top level branches onto a bright balcony that is further divided into two private alcoves. Another alcove is reserved for the practice of the Korean Tea Ceremony.

Franchia sets aside two hours for their prix fixe Royal Tea Tray—a suitable time within an otherwise hectic business day for a serene intermission, and time enough to indulge in a special menu of vegetarian appetizers and mini-desserts.

Tea at Franchia is presented in a little white pot bearing the inscription: "Tea and Zen are one and the same." As importers of fine teas from all over Asia, Franchia presents a wide selection, but most noteworthy of course are their Korean Wild Green Teas from several pickings. The most extensive range of teas encompasses thirteen herbals, such as Chrysanthemum, Organic Dandelion, and Ginger and Ginseng.

A wall cubby displays a collection of Korean-made teacups and strainers, tea-leaf containers, tea scoops, and five-person tea sets, all of which are for sale—as are Franchia's brand of loose-leaf teas. Everything on the menu can be ordered to go, as well.

the gallery

AT THE CARLYLE HOTEL

33 East 76th Street
bet. Madison and Park Avenues

or Madison Avenue
bet. 76th and 77th Streets

212-744-1600

www.thecarlyle.com

Hours: Daily 3 P.M. to 5:30 P.M.

Price Range: $$$

Locating the Gallery is something of an adventure as neither of the two entrances into the Carlyle Hotel immediately suggests its presence. Your best bet is to enter the hotel from Madison Avenue and proceed through Bemelmans Bar—pause to look at the delicious murals by the illustrator of the beloved Madeline books, and take note that the bar offers a children's tea (see page 121).

The Gallery is an anteroom to the hotel restaurant. Designed by Italian architect Renzo Mongiardino, the Gallery is an octagon flattered by exuberant hand-painted wallpapers by Milanese artist Enrico Brusi, which are said to evoke the Sultan's dining room in Istanbul's Tokapi Palace. In keeping with the sultan/harem theme, comfy banquettes are upholstered in antique kilims; these are complemented by fringe-trimmed red-velvet armchairs and charming poufs with basket-weave bases.

The three-course afternoon tea is presented all at once on a tiered stand displaying a selection of tea sandwiches, crumpets served with Devonshire cream and preserves, and miniature pastries. For those who do not wish to partake of three full courses, everything may be ordered à la carte.

The Gallery prides itself on its repertoire of teas—there are fourteen of these—as well as a medley of sherries and ports by the glass and champagnes by the bottle. In addition, it offers a 'specialty afternoon cocktail' called The Earl Grey MarTEAni, which is composed of gin "infused with Earl Grey tea, lemon juice, simple syrup, and egg white."

garden court café

AT ASIA SOCIETY AND MUSEUM

725 Park Avenue
bet. 70th and 71st Streets
212-570-5202
www.asiasociety.org
Hours: Tuesday through Sunday 3:15 P.M.
to 4 P.M.
Price Range: $$

In the city, one of the loveliest places to spend time is the serene Asia Society. "Dedicated to fostering understanding of Asia and communication between Americans and the peoples of Asia and the Pacific," the society (and its museum) was founded in 1956 by John D. Rockefeller, III.

The institution moved into its present building, designed by Edward Larrabee Barnes, in 1981. A few years ago, an overhaul of the building by architect Bartholomew Voorsanger resulted in a number of architectural delights, one being the glass staircase leading to and from the galleries, and another being the Garden Café, a dramatic yet tranquil glass-enclosed space that appears to lean into 70th Street. Tables share this airy room with five delicate, weeping podocarpus trees.

Taking tea here—or a meal—is a sensuous experience. Teas, which are served in traditional Asian teapots, are from SerendipiTea and bear delightful names: Once Upon A Time, for instance, blends hints of chocolate, mint, and vanilla with rooibos, while Ruby Slipper is an herbal that might waft you on a delightful flight of fancy (to Oz, perhaps?). Desserts change seasonally, but always include a plate of homemade cookies and ginger and green tea ice cream.

If you become enamored of your teapot, Asia Store across the lobby stocks an extensive range, including Chinese Yixing clay teapots, Japanese cast-iron pots with warming stands, as well as wooden tea ceremony boxes, bamboo scoops, and whisks.

the gotham lounge

AT THE PENINSULA HOTEL

700 Fifth Avenue
entrance on West 55th Street
bet. Fifth and Sixth Avenues
212-247-2200
www.newyork.peninsula.com
Hours: Daily 2:30 P.M. to 5 P.M.
Price Range: $$$

Steps up from the Peninsula's chandelier-lit lobby, the Gotham Lounge provides a quiet sense of delicious privacy, both for hotel guests and for visitors strolling in from shopping or a matinee. Here, conversation is muted by plush carpeting and luxuriant draperies at the arched windows, which gaze upon the chocolate walls of Fifth Avenue Presbyterian Church across the street. Walls, painted to simulate tawny stone, provide a 'High Renaissance' backdrop for framed frescoes depicting Arcadian landscapes and luminous, oversized photographs of leather-bound books. Two tables are inlaid with game boards, should you decide to engage in chess or checkers while you sip your tea.

The tea selection is concise. Five are blended specifically for the Peninsula Hotel in Hong Kong; another seven, including a blend called Chameleon, are imported from Taylor's of Harrogate, in England.

The four courses of the prix fixe afternoon tea, served on delicate Wedgwood china, include an exotic assortment of finger sandwiches, such as roast beef with Boursin cream cheese, horseradish, and asparagus salad on whole-wheat bread, herb-roasted shrimp and roasted tomato hummus on toast, and smoked salmon with caviar and crème fraîche.

Scones with Devonshire clotted cream and preserves follow, then a selection of tea breads and English pound cake with lemon curd, then mini fruit tartlets and chocolate pastries. If that isn't enough, let a glass of Louis Roederer Brut champagne extend your repast into the happy hour.

the harlem tea room

1793A Madison Avenue
bet. 117th and 118th Streets
212-348-3471
www.harlemtearoom.com
Hours: Saturday, two seatings at 1 P.M. and
3:30 P.M.
Price Range: $$

When she graduated from business school, Patrice Clayton knew she wanted to "give back" to the Harlem neighborhood she calls home. Always fascinated by the mystique of all things tea, she decided to open a tearoom in an area that has experienced a renaissance, especially in row-house construction. The new brick dwellings along this stretch of Madison Avenue and its adjacent streets create a picturesque backdrop to this charming gathering spot, especially on Saturday afternoons when the Harlem Tea Room presents its prix fixe Proper Afternoon Tea. Judging from the chatter overheard at every table, Patrice has succeeded in contributing to the sense of renewed vitality in her neighborhood.

The generously scaled space is painted a warm mustard-ochre; banquettes are clad in burgundy-and-gold tapestry; and deep burgundy draperies hang at the big plate-glass windows, which harness the warmth of the afternoon sun. Dining chairs are cozily upholstered in suede-cloth and mahogany-toned tables are set with gold-rimmed white china. A rock-crystal sugar stick rests upon every saucer.

The tea service offers an array of finger sandwiches, including curried chicken, classic cucumber, egg salad, sun-dried tomato with goat cheese, and smoked salmon with cream cheese. Warm scones, accompanied by whipped cream and preserves and a plate of cookies, complete the three-course affair. The roster of twenty-six teas includes Oriental Fantasy, Caribbean Dreams, and Amor' Paris. As a less filling alternative to the full tea, you can opt for the Cream Tea, which includes a tea of your choice plus assorted scones.

The Harlem Tea Room also hosts myriad events, including a Jazz Tea with live music.

kai

AT ITO EN

822 Madison Avenue
bet. 68th and 69th Streets
212-988-7277
www.itoen.com
Hours: Tuesday through Saturday 2:30 P.M.
    to 4:15 P.M.
Price Range: $$

Sharing the harmony and hospitality evoked by the Japanese tea ceremony, but without the esoteric formalities, is the avowed aim of Kai, the restaurant that shares its Madison Avenue premises with Ito En, a purveyor of fine, artisanal teas and tea things, mainly from Japan.

Kai, located upstairs from the shop, is discreetly compartmentalized into two areas: a narrow sushi bar in back behind a gauzy curtain; and the more commodious yet still intimate restaurant up front, which is open for lunch and dinner as well as afternoon tea. The room cantilevers over the teashop below, protected by a wide glass rail that looks out through double-height windows onto Madison Avenue. Banquettes upholstered the shade of silver-tipped tea leaves, black tables set with black slabs of slate in lieu of fabric placemats, and black chairs set off the myriad colors and textures of the food.

'Kai' means gathering place; the word is also short for *kaiseki*, the delicate little nibbles that enhance the tea ceremony. Kai's prix fixe Zen Tea presents a pot of tea with an array of nine sweets on a tiered dessert stand. The Matcha Tea teams matcha (a drink linked historically to the tea ceremony, made from fine, powdered green tea leaves with an intensely sweet and deep flavor) with a dessert of your choice from an à la carte menu—matcha-covered almonds and a tiny meringue accompany the sweet.

Five Japanese teas head the menu, followed by select teas from China, India, and Sri Lanka, an array of tisanes, and two florals. Estio, a Chinese green tea, is flavored with yuzu (an East Asian citrus fruit), apricot, lemongrass, and bergamot, while the cheerful Ding Dong tea is, as advertised, mellow. All teas are poured from artisanal pots into tiny handle-less cups, which rest upon bronzed leaves instead of coasters.

keko café

GOURMET COFFEE & TEA HOUSE

121 Madison Avenue
bet. 30th and 31st Streets
212-685-4360
Hours: Daily 2:30 P.M. to 6 P.M.
Price Range: $

Although it is located across the street from the American Academy of Dramatic Arts, which was designed by the celebrated architect Stanford White, the diminutive Keko Café inhabits an unprepossessing stretch of lower Madison Avenue that is otherwise dedicated to showrooms for rug merchants and other less "dramatic" trades.

A charming grandmother's attic of a tearoom, Keko enchants, its front door garlanded with ivy and its windows softened with ruffled lace. Inside, walls covered with architectural engravings, botanical prints, and urban scenes, sundry cubbies and shelves packed to overflowing with teaware, découpaged boxes, and suitcases contribute to an atmosphere of congenial intimacy.

Leaf teas—there are almost two dozen in stock—are displayed behind the pastry counter, and you can choose any one for your in-house pot of tea. Some exotic varieties to note are an Indian Spice black tea, a Moroccan green, Egyptian chamomile, and an hibiscus floral blend. During the weekday rush hours, Keko serves a walk-in/take-out and delivery clientele, but during the mid- to late afternoon, tranquility reigns at the café's handful of petite copper-topped tables.

Tea can be enjoyed in the traditional three-course "Tea Time" style, with tea sandwiches, freshly baked scones, and sweets. If your appetite is not up to the challenge of a full repast, you can order à la carte. Sweets include chocolate mousse cake, cheesecake, carrot cake, torta della nonna, granny's cake, tiramisu, and gelati.

knit new york

307 East 14th Street
bet. Second and First Avenues
212-387-0707
www.knitnewyork.com
Hours: Daily 11 A.M. to 8 P.M.
Price Range: $

New York is a city of aficionados—of opera, theater, film, and dance, of home teams like the Yankees and the Mets, and of—well, name any hobby or pursuit and you'll find a band of like-minded fans somewhere in town. Crafts of all kinds find their niche in New York, too, from making paper to piecing quilts and knitting.

Thus, Knit New York. When you step down off the sidewalk into this shop-cum-workshop, you find yourself surrounded by a virtual rainbow of colorful yarns in every width and weight. At the back of the gallery is an intimate nook where knitting classes are held, and yet another room behind that packed floor to ceiling with yarn.

Where does taking tea fit into all this? Along one wall, Knit New York set up a beverage bar, which offers seventeen healthful SerendipiTeas, including Temple of Heavens Gunpowder Green, Cassis Black, Yerba Mate Tisane, and myriad shades in between. Balthazar Bakery supplies fresh croissants daily, and there is also a selection of plump muffins and scones.

Six tables run alongside the yarn display wall, each flanked by a pair of Arne Jacobsen–style chairs. While oldies' music croons in the background, you can peruse Knit New York's wide selection of books and magazines dedicated to knitting, or purchase a pattern book to study on your own as you sip your tea—and knit.

Knit New York offers a schedule of knitting classes—at all levels—plus a Sox & Lox Sunday lesson that includes all materials for making socks, and an orange juice and bagel brunch. The shop also offers private knitting lessons, and is available to cater private parties, too.

lady m

41 East 78th Street
bet. Madison and Park Avenues
212-452-2222
www.ladymconfections.com
Hours: Monday through Friday 9 A.M. to 8 P.M.;
  Saturday 10 A.M. to 8 P.M.; Sunday 10 A.M. to
  6 P.M.
Price Range: $$

Slid like a drawer into an Upper East Side yellow-brick façade, the sleek, oblong white-on-white slice of a café-and-cake boutique that is Lady M is the quintessential showcase for a confectioner's—and tea lover's—connoisseurship and panache. Designed by Sam Trimble, who won an architectural competition to design this space, the room and its assorted pastries appear as creamy and delectable as a Wayne Thibault painting. Cakes and sweets are displayed like exquisite jewelry on glass stands and crisp rectangles of monogrammed white baking paper in a long case crafted from interleaved strips of white-quartz aggregrate and onyx inspired by the shop's signature twenty-one-layer Mille Crêpes dessert.

White tables and chairs are set out along the wall opposite the cake display, with another pair positioned at the back of the shop. Here, you can sit and sample a dessert along with one of the boutique's half-dozen blended teas: Chai Berry, Green Splendour, Assam, Lady M Grey, Lady M Herbal, and Creamy Morning, which the staff says is everyone's favorite because it releases a tantalizing caramel aroma.

Tea is served in a rotund teapot shaped like a fat macaroon. Buttercream in hue, the teapot, like its matching teacup, was commissioned by Lady M from Limoges and sports a gleaming gold handle as bright as a wedding ring.

A final note: All desserts can be made to order and for take-out, and Lady M caters as well.

lady mendl's tea salon

AT THE INN AT IRVING PLACE

56 Irving Place
bet. 15th and 16th Streets
212-533-4466
www.innatirving.com
Hours: Seatings Wednesday through Friday
at 3 P.M. and 5 P.M.; Saturday and Sunday at
2 P.M. and 4:30 P.M.; reservations required.
Price Range: $$$

Of all the tea venues in Manhattan, none is more in thrall to the elegant experience of taking tea than Lady Mendl's Tea Salon, which occupies the parlor floor in one of the city's handsomest hostelries, the Inn at Irving Place, a few blocks south of Gramercy Park.

Somewhat idiosyncratically, the salon is named after one of America's pioneering interior decorators, Elsie de Wolfe (later Lady Mendl), who became famous when she cast aside the fripperies of Victoriana to create pale, uncluttered rooms, free of geegaws and the like.

The Tea Salon, however, fully endorses Victoriana, but in a far more romantic vein than the overstuffed interiors Elsie excoriated. Would Elsie approve of this room? Would she be seduced by it? She was a great party-giver, so one wonders. At any rate, extravagance prevails, not only in the lush décor but in the tea service as well. The salon offers its prix fixe tea service at two seatings and presents, with considerable flourish and aplomb, not a mere three-course tea but a full-blown five-course repast consisting of a taste of seasonal fruits followed by tea sandwiches, scones, sweets and candied citrus peels, and, finally, a lavish wedge of dacquoise, a decadent sandwich of buttercream between meringues.

The choice of tea is equally rich—close to three dozen—and includes iced teas during the summer months. So why not forget lunch and dinner and settle in for the afternoon? It is quite a treat, and one worth climbing the front steps for. After all, if you're not staying at the inn, you can call a taxi—or a pedicab—to roll you home.

le salon de thé

AT LA MAISON DU CHOCOLAT

1018 Madison Avenue
bet. 77th and 78th Streets
212-744-7117

www.lamaisonduchocolat.com

Hours: Monday through Saturday 10 A.M. to

6 P.M.; Sunday Noon to 5 P.M.

Price Range: $$

Even though this is a book devoted to tea, I have been known to sip other potables. Deflated by mid-morning blahs, for instance, I often pop into a coffee shop for an espresso macchiato. And then there's hot chocolate! For this, I am irresistibly drawn to La Maison du Chocolat, run by an esteemed chocolatier from France who thoughtfully added a delicious little chocolate box of a café behind this Upper East Side boutique. Here, walls painted a golden hue and chocolate-toned carpeting set off the café's stand-up bar and half-dozen diminutive tables—and mute conversation to a pleasurable purr.

The five teas on the salon menu reflect a pre-cise and refined sensibility. There's a tawny Darjeel-ing from the Makaibari Estate in the Himalayas, a Ceylon New Vithanakande Estate, a mélange blended—and named—for the boutique, which is infused with the essences of seven different citrus fruits, a gunpowder green, and a rooibos with a hint of vanilla from South Africa.

The raison d'etre of the café, of course, is its seductive menu of patisseries. Flavored mousse cakes—Delice, Andalousie, and Maracuja, among others—feel as luxuriant to the palette as their mellifluous names sound to the ear. Equally generous are plump macaroons in two sizes, as well as La Maison's self-styled degustation platter consisting of seven pieces of chocolate. And what about hot chocolate? There are two—a silky Guayaquil and a full-bodied Caracas—and they are superb!

La Maison du Chocolat has a shop (but no café) at 30 Rockefeller Plaza, and offers monthly chocolate-tasting sessions billed as "Le Parcours Initiatique."

the lobby lounge

AT THE FOUR SEASONS HOTEL, NEW YORK

57 East 57th Street
bet. Madison and Park Avenues
212-758-5700
www.fourseasons.com/newyorkfs
Hours: Daily 2 P.M. to 5 P.M.
Price Range: $$$

The Four Seasons' Lobby Lounge and companion restaurant have undergone a renovation that is at once spiffy and discreet. In the afternoons, the two-story-high lounge, up a low flight of stairs at the left of the spacious entrance hall, offers an Afternoon Tea Celebration—a prix fixe affair that segues neatly into cocktail hour.

During the winter, a mammoth fireplace beckons at the Fifty-Seventh Street end of the lounge. Here, window tables observe the hustle and bustle of shoppers and trippers parading outside. Conversation islands beckon groups of any size—several are geared to large parties, with multi-seat sofas facing deep curved armchairs, while tables for two naturally invite intimate tête-à-têtes. Toasty, honey-colored carpeting offsets warm green upholstery to flattering effect, and as a dramatic counterpoint to the restful scene, enormous floral arrangements flare from massive silvery urns.

The tea service itself, overseen by executive chef Brooke Vosika and executive pastry chef Michael Mignano, comprises a choice of three savories (a.k.a. tea sandwiches) from a line-up of eight, three sweets, and apple-cinnamon scones accompanied by an assortment of jams and Devonshire cream. Check out the American Caviar Chive Purse and Lobster Salad on Brioche with Tarragon and Watercress. Besides pastries, there are also toasted amaretto cookies and ginger oatmeal shortbread. One teacake, a dark chocolate, is scented with Earl Grey tea.

Teas, from a company called 'T' in British Columbia, number seventeen. Only one is exclusive to the hotel: an apple rooibos. Others include a Sencha Fukujyu Cha green and a black called, improbably, Pannetone. Should you decide to stay on for drinks, four of them—a vodka, a gin and tonic, and two martinis—are infused with hints of tea.

the lobby lounge

AT THE MANDARIN ORIENTAL, NEW YORK

80 Columbus Circle
at 60th Street bet. Broadway and Ninth
Avenue

212-805-8800

www.mandarinoriental.com

Hours: Daily 2:30 P.M. to 5 P.M.

Price Range: $$$

The replacement of the abandoned Coliseum on Columbus Circle with the impressive glass towers of the Time Warner Center provided a just cause for celebration. Today, the center is a major tourist destination, not only for its indoor shopping mall but also for its acclaimed restaurants. Here, too, starting at the thirty-fifth floor of the north tower, is a suitably grand hotel: the Mandarin Oriental New York.

Elevators ascend to the lobby either from the hotel's main entrance on 60th Street or from the third floor in the mall. Exiting the elevators, you find yourself facing a dramatically-lit glass sculpture by famed glass artist Dale Chihuly, which is 'planted' in a bed of moss. The bi-level lobby lounge beyond offers a breathtaking view through a bank of windows to Central Park South, Columbus Circle, the south end of the park, and a dazzling skyline.

The lounge is thoughtfully laid out with seating groups in various configurations to accommodate parties of virtually any size. Banquettes, armchairs clad in striped velvet or blond leather, and big granite-topped tables offer plenty of room for the prix fixe afternoon tea service—or for drinks or snacks from an ample room service-style menu.

The Mandarin Oriental's dozen teas include two special blends with essences of the mandarin fruit itself. Scones are complemented by Devonshire cream and "house-made marmalade," and honey supplements sugar as a tea sweetener. Tea sandwiches are twice the normal size, while sweets, by pastry chef Paul Nolan, range from a properly dippable Proustian madeleine to miniature shortbread squares and a tiny chocolate cup. Everything is so delicious you may find yourself wishing time would simply stop on the illuminated CNN sign outside the window.

the lobby lounge

AT THE RITZ-CARLTON HOTEL,
BATTERY PARK

2 West Street at Battery Place

212-344-0800

www.ritzcarlton.com

Hours: Monday through Saturday 2 P.M. to
5 P.M.

Price Range: $$$

Located as it is in the financial hub of Manhattan, the Ritz-Carlton—on the upper fringe of Battery Bark, across from Castle Clinton—decided to call its traditional, prix fixe afternoon service Power Tea. On a recent visit, a pair of hip-hop types were imbibing champagne, while two businessmen, stopping in on their way to the airport, made do with a quick coffee while they parried urgent last-minute calls on their cell phones. So much for tradition.

That said, the airy, two-story Art Deco-style lounge (which adjoins Two West Restaurant) looks out to handsome views of the harbor and the Hudson River. Comfort is assured with sink-into loveseats, handsome chairs clad in striped velvet, and tables big enough to accommodate the triple-tiered array of tea sandwiches, breads, madeleines, scones, and pastries, as well as silver-plated sternos, which keep teapots warm. A separate tray holds honey and sweeteners.

Colors in the room are soft, from honey-toned wood walls to sage-fog-and-gold upholstery to pale yellow Wedgwood china featuring borders flecked with sprigs of field flowers and yellow and grey damask linens. Sprays of miniature orchids add a festive accent to the table settings.

The tea selection is limited, but refined. Besides the usual line-up, there is a delicate blend exclusive to the hotel called Blue Sapphire Afternoon Tea, as well as a brisk Hajua Estate Tippy Assam, and a gunpowder green. Sandwich fillings include fresh tuna, foie gras, caviar, and salmon on a slice of cucumber, while sweets include a miniature fruit tart, a lemon curd tart, ladyfingers, and, as a fillip, little pots made of chocolate filled with crème fraîche, raspberry jam, and pistachio crème.

mcnally robinson booksellers

52 Prince Street
bet. Mulberry and Lafayette Streets
212-274-1160

www.mcnallyrobinsonnyc.com

Hours: Monday through Saturday 10 A.M. to
10 P.M.; Sunday 10 A.M. to 9 P.M.

Price Range: $

When Susan McNally decided that she wanted to open an independent bookstore-cum-tearoom a few years ago, she zeroed in on NoLita, an area of the city that was still—as a Webmaster might say—"under construction." Nearby SoHo pulsated with tourists, but NoLita was, if not a backwater, then surely one of the quieter enclaves in town.

No more. Like the East Village and the Lower East Side, NoLita is hopping, and McNally Robinson is the beneficiary of many said hoppers, who pop in to buy a book and to relax over a cup of tea and something to eat. The street-plus-basement shop is laid out in a comfortable and orderly fashion, with fanny-friendly stools and one inviting, lolling chaise. The tearoom, with its copper-topped tables, is embraced by a curve of wall that welcomes customers like a friendly hug. One long, chunky wooden table is flanked by benches, perfect for groups. WiFi is also available, with a purchase of something to eat or drink.

Teas are listed on a chalkboard. Besides English Breakfast and Earl Grey, there's a honey-like ceylon, a chai masala, a "Five o'Clock blend" of Darjeeling, ceylon and oolong leaves, and blackcurrant. "Summer breeze," which mingles berries and fruits, begs to be poured over ice. Each tea can be ramped up with a healthful Tea Aid that claims to assist in maintaining immunity or memory, act as an antidote to allergies or the flu, or help relieve a hangover. Gowiths include "Bites" such as toast, scones, and muffins, and "Sweet Bites," which include the three C's—chocolate cake, cupcakes, and cookies—as well as brownies and biscotti. Just don't drop crumbs into a book you don't intend to buy.

the morgan café

225 Madison Avenue
bet. 36th and 37th Streets
212-683-0008
www.morganlibrary.org
Hours: Tuesday through Thursday 11 A.M. to
    4 P.M.; Friday 11 A.M. to 8 P.M.;
    Saturday 11 A.M. to 5 P.M.
Price Range: $$

After several years in renovation mode, the Morgan Library emerged from under wraps with a new name and a completely new look. As the Morgan Library & Museum, its various independent buildings have been masterfully refreshed and reconfigured by Italian architect Renzo Piano, who linked the scattered mélange of historic spaces with a soaring central court of glass and metal. From here you can fan out in different directions to take in the Morgan's many treasures, including financier J.P. Morgan's original study and library and several galleries, as well as an elegant dining room and a gift shop.

The Gilbert Court is also the site of The Morgan Café, which occupies one corner of the airy space. The café presents a comprehensive menu throughout the day. Best of all, it has revived the Morgan Afternoon Tea (which can be ordered anytime). The prix fixe, three-course repast includes the usual line-up of finger sandwiches, scones, and pastries, including a fruit tartlet. More wonderfully still, executive chef Charlene Shade has reintroduced the institution's signature Laura Morgan sugar cookies. Teas are from the Harney & Sons line of Premier Sachet Teas.

Tea can be taken on its own, too, with a decadent delight such as molten chocolate cake with Tahitian vanilla ice cream and blackberry coulis, or lemon soufflé glacé with macerated peppered strawberries.

payard patisserie & bistro

1032 Lexington Avenue
bet. 73rd and 74th Streets
212-717-5252
www.payard.com
Hours: Monday through Saturday 3:30 P.M.
   to 5 P.M.
Price Range: $$

Award-winning pastry chef Francois Payard's luxe
eatery emerged like a phoenix from a graffiti-scarred
storefront on the Upper East Side. On this inauspi-
cious site, M. Payard created what must be every
Francophile's fantasy of a Parisian patisserie: even the
windows facing the street advertise his confectionary
flair and ingenuity. Seasonal displays of elaborate
multi-tiered cakes and other treats stand poised like
sweet sentries to either side of the front door. Just
inside, enormous cases are filled with every sinful
indulgence you have ever dreamt of, from tiny truffles
to cakes named for famous monuments and chateaux
in France.

Payard is zoned into three comfortable chocolate
and buttercream-colored spaces. Embraced by the
pastry cases, the entry area hosts a snug coffee and
wine bar, as well as half a dozen café tables with
crackled orange tops, which are encircled on the floor
by an inlaid mosaic ring that features a series of 'float-

ing' teacups. At the rear of the patisserie is a softly-lit bi-level bistro. Tables on the balcony wear table-cloths; those below are bare.

The formal prix fixe afternoon tea at Payard is lavish and offers original and sumptuous variations on the traditional Anglo theme. Sandwiches, for example, include a vitello tonnato on ciabatta bread, while the scones course includes—how very Proustian!—madeleines. The more expansive menu for Payard's Thé Royal adds caviar and blinis and a plate of crème de mare to the three-course meal. All teas are special blends: you make your selection from several blacks, a green sencha, and three "fantasies," each of which is flavored with fruit.

the pembroke room

AT THE LOWELL HOTEL

28 East 63rd Street
bet. Madison and Park Avenues
212-838-1400
www.lowellhotel.com
Hours: Daily 3 P.M. to 6 P.M.
Price Range: $$$

This elegant hat-and-gloves dowager of a tearoom turns quietly inward and focuses on the simple delight of enjoying afternoon tea without interruption or distraction. Swag-and-jabot window treatments in appropriately 'tea-stained' chintz trimmed with tri-colored tassels and lace under-curtains camouflage the fact that the Pembroke Room does not entertain a view to the outdoors. But that does not matter, because light diffused through the lace is amplified by mirrors, which are themselves anchored with crystal sconces that sparkle and shimmer, casting a warm glow. Best of all, there is no noise from traffic outside.

During the hours dedicated to the Lowell's afternoon tea, comfortable Louis XV-style oval-backed armchairs pull up around tables set with blue-and-gold rimmed china and footed silver-plate salvers holding a collection of Wilkin & Sons marmalade and jams. Once you have chosen your tea—from a selection of twenty-one, including two oolongs, an herbal blend called Harmony, and the Lowell's own Hotel Blend—tea and hot water are poured from silver-plated pots whose handles are thoughtfully protected by diminutive tea cozies.

The three-course menu is presented sequentially: a half-dozen tea sandwiches followed by a large currant scone accompanied by a bowl of strawberries and clotted cream, and, finally, by a tiered stand displaying an array of tiny sweets, including one level dedicated entirely to cookies.

With all this peace and quiet, it is a pleasure to draw out teatime for as long as possible.

the petrie court

AT THE METROPOLITAN MUSEM OF ART

1000 Fifth Avenue
bet. 80th and 84th Streets
212-879-5500
www.metmuseum.org
Hours: Sunday and Tuesday through
Thursday 2:30 P.M. to 4:30 P.M.; Friday and
Saturday 2:30 P.M. to 5 P.M.
Price Range: $$

With unerring foresight, the Metropolitan Museum of Art, through various renovations, has created several separate handsome venues where visitors can have a bite to eat. In addition, the sculpture garden on the roof, open during warm weather months, offers iced tea.

Tea—presented as a bag in a generous mug—and munchies are available in the new cafeteria located in the basement (access by elevator or stairs adjacent to the Lehman Wing), as well as at the Balcony Café overlooking the Great Hall.

For a lovely "French-inspired Afternoon Tea" with solicitous waiter service, though, the place to go is the Petrie Court Café. This airy space, with its double-height window wall overlooking the lawn and Egyptian obelisk behind the museum, is the perfect spot for a spot. Select a tea from a dozen blended by Harney & Sons. Tempting treats to accompany a brew include miniature savories (croque monsieur, zucchini quiche, and smoked salmon or spinach crepe); a mini-brioche with strawberry butter, lemon curd, and wild blueberry and peach preserves; and an assortment of petite tarts, as well as a puffy macaroon and candied orange zest.

For an additional fee, you can add a flute of Pommery Brut champagne to your meal. Luckily, the bronze Rodin torsos in the cafe are headless, so they won't gape as you stagger away after your filling of tea to take in more of the Met's incomparable wealth of treasures.

Exalted categories of members to the museum can ascend to the elegant Patrons' Lounge on the fourth floor to partake of afternoon tea there: same hours, same menu.

podunk tearoom

231 East 5th Street
bet. Cooper Square and Second Avenue
212-677-7722

Hours: Tuesday through Sunday 11 A.M. to
9 P.M.

Price Range: $$

Happening upon Podunk during a stroll through the
East Village is like stumbling into Oz: Poof! All at once
you are at a remove from the black-and-white grit of
the city and whisked into the colorful countryside.
From its perky yellow-and-white striped awning to its
cheerful miscellany of flea-market furnishings, Podunk
promotes bucolic bliss.

Overseen by owner and baker Elspeth Treadwell
and her husband, Podunk opens its arms—and its
heart—in a neighborly hug. Elspeth says the tearoom,
which she opened in 2002, is her family's "country
home," and its informal atmosphere gives the impres-
sion that you are sharing her idyll—an impression
reinforced by the sight of her childrens' scooters
parked under a desk near the bakery counter at the
rear of the room.

For Elspeth, tea is everything. Tea and baked
goodies, which she improvises "by smell and taste"
might be varied as the mood strikes her. Indeed, each
entry on the menu is a mini tea menu in itself: there

are eighteen of these, all yummy and comforting. Tea & Tarts heads the list and partners a savory tart of the day with two dessert tartlets and osmanthus green tea; Tittle-Tattle Tea is composed of Lady Black tea with a cupcake and cookies; and two teas, served only on weekends, are actually brunches.

Elspeth classifies teatime as "interactive," and she does not accept gratuities. The customer really does the work, she says: sniffing at a canister of tea; pouring from one of Podunk's generous collections of teapots; carrying one's tray to a table; and, of course, digging in. One bench is aptly called the "bus stop"—here, visitors can peruse the menu, check out the goodies on display, and consult Elspeth about which tea would satisfy.

rma café

AT THE RUBIN MUSEUM OF ART

150 West 17th Street
bet. Sixth and Seventh Avenues
212-620-5000
www.rmanyc.org
Hours: 11:30 A.M. until one-half hour before
    museum closing; closed Tuesdays.
Price Range: $$

One of New York's gems is the museum founded by Donald and Shelley Rubin comprising art from the Himalayas and surrounding areas, which the couple has amassed over the past four decades. This collection of Asian art has been cited as the largest in the Western world.

According to RMA's brochure, the Rubins were "determined to share their collection with the public" and, to that end, purchased and renovated the old Barneys department store to house their art. Calling upon Barneys' architectural firm, Beyer Blinder Belle, and designer Milton Glaser, the Rubins created a space that educates and welcomes in a variety of ways, including outreach efforts such as RMA Café, which converts to the casual K2Lounge during happy hour—and at others to a Cabaret Cinema.

Two centerpieces of the museum, visible from the entrance, are a striking, six-story stainless-steel coil of a stair created by French designer Andree Put-man for Barneys, and the sinuous copper *Dream Screen* by Milton Glaser behind the admissions desk. Immediately to the left of these is the colonnade and café, with well-spaced cherry tables and an informal service bar. Items described on the menu are displayed with labels, museum-style, along the bar.

One of the signature features of RMA Café is its tea menu—this includes a Japanese genmaicha green made from bancha tea and popped roasted rice, a Nantou oolong, an orange pekoe from Ceylon, a sweet, aromatic black known as Dragon Eyes, and two herbals. The selection of snacks and nibbles runs the gamut from green tea wasabi-coated peanuts to pumpkin and apple breads and cookies emblazoned with the museum logo and a "dragon demon."

sanctuary t

337B West Broadway
bet. Broome and Grand Streets

212-941-STEA (7832)

www.sanctuarytea.com

Hours: Daily 8 A.M. to midnight

Price Range: $

Sanctuary T, one of New York's newest and freshest tea venues, was conceived by its founder, Dawn Cameron, as an e-tail operation, selling specially blended teas and home and beauty products with tea as a theme or ingredient. Opening a restaurant seemed a logical next step, and the new place is a soothing spot; with padded (walls and ceiling alike) in Assam-toned cork to counteract the usual trendy din, it seats just forty, overflowing in warm weather onto a space open to the sidewalk. Sanctuary T wares are on display in narrow wall insets and along shelves at the back, and are worth inspection—they include custom-mixed loose blends in glass bottles accompanied by little wooden scoops hanging in silken sacks.

Overseen by consultant Aleksandra Milicevic, chef Kevin Stanton, and drinks mixologist Benoit Cornet, Sanctuary T serves three meals a day, as well as teas, and artfully employs favorite infusions as significant ingredients in many of its innovative sips and bites, including several cocktails and "small plates for sharing." The simplest cocktail is titled Quintessence: Earl Grey sluiced with gin and soda, plus a splash of lime. A dozen blends are recommended as dessert teas, and two desserts are accented with tea.

The selection of teas and infusions is large—there are more than fifty—and wide-ranging. The menu is posted on a huge blackboard behind the bar, one end of which is set apart for Sanctuary T's self-styled tea ceremony. Here you can pinch and sniff and observe your chosen leaves brewing in a striking glass decanter, monitored by a custom-crafted timer set in a wood cube. The baristas will also make up tea bags to order. In-house tea can be taken in a glass mug or, if two or four decide to share the same tea, it will appear in a decanter with a built-in tea light to maintain the proper temperature. Wi-Fi access, board games, and magazines are also on hand for those who want to hang out for a spell.

sarabeth's

AT THE WALES HOTEL

1295 Madison Avenue
bet. 91st and 92nd Streets
212-410-7335
www.sarabeths.com
Hours: Daily 3:30 P.M. to 5:30 P.M.
Price Range: $$

It seems hard to believe, but Sarabeth's on Madison Avenue—a longtime must on the Sunday brunch and ladies-who-lunch circuit—has been around for a quarter of a century. Housed in Carnegie Hill's chummy, Anglophile, country-in-the-city Wales Hotel, Sarabeth's opened back in 1983 as an outgrowth of a thriving business in jams, preserves, and baked goods started by the eponymous Sarabeth and her husband, Bill Levine. The enterprise has grown steadily over the years; today, the franchise includes a café in the basement of the Whitney Museum of American Art and a bakery in the Chelsea Market, as well as two additional Sarabeth's restaurant/tearooms—one on Amsterdam Avenue and one on Central Park South (see pages 131–132).

A no-reservations restaurant, Sarabeth's is usually queue-crazed during lunch and weekend brunch—some days you can barely penetrate the crowd on the sidewalk. A much saner time to bask in Sarabeth's hospitality is teatime.

Pale-yellow walls highlighted by painterly land-scapes, tapestry-clad banquettes, commodious tables, and grandly scaled chandeliers invite lingering over afternoon tea—be it the prix fixe three-course version or just a piping hot pot of tea and a delicious Sarabeth's home-baked scone, a plate of delicate cookies, or a sinful sweet from the pastry case—which, like Sarabeth's jams and preserves, can also be purchased separately to take home.

the star lounge

AT THE RITZ-CARLTON HOTEL,
CENTRAL PARK

50 Central Park South
bet. Fifth and Sixth Avenues
212-308-9100
www.ritzcarlton.com
Hours: Daily 2:30 P.M. to 5 P.M.
Price Range: $$$

A number of years ago, the venerable Ritz-Carlton Hotel purchased and renovated the landmark St. Moritz Hotel at the corner of Sixth Avenue on Central Park South. A highlight of the refurbished space is the Star Lounge, which is located beyond the lobby. Completely paneled—walls and ceilings alike—in mellow, fine-burled anigre wood from South Carolina, the lounge features paintings from the private collection of Millennium Partners, owners of the hotel, which contribute to the library-like intimacy of the room. Large, watery landscapes conveying lyrical reflections on peace and harmony are by artist and set-designer Stephen Hannock; post-impressionist urban scenes are by Samuel Halpert, who worked both in New York City and in Europe during the early twentieth century.

In the lounge, comfortable islands of repose include loveseats upholstered in aqua damask and skirted with fat bullion fringe; armchairs of various styles wearing textiles in compatible tones; and expansive tables set with yellow placemats and Wedgwood china. Settings are enhanced by little fish-bowl-style vases, each floating a single full-blown rose, and tiny trays thoughtfully stocked with sweet-eners, honey, and lemon wedges.

The prix fixe afternoon tea comes as a leisurely sequence of courses, rather than all at once. For this reason, plan on lingering, so you can luxuriate in the delicacies prepared by Alain Allegretti, executive chef at the Ritz-Carlton's restaurant Atelier. Tea sand-wiches present an original twist on traditional fare: crab, for example, nestles within a lemon-filled éclair on a chive baton. Tea can also be ordered à la carte or to share.

subtletea

121 Madison Avenue
at 30th Street
212-481-4713
www.subtletea.com
Hours: Monday through Friday 6:30 A.M. to
8 P.M.; Saturday 7 A.M. to 7 P.M.;
Sunday 8 A.M. to 6 P.M.
Price Range: $

When brothers and co-entrepreneurs Todd and Tim Cella opened SubtleTea, it immediately drew crowds—not only for its take-out menu and takeaway teas (fifty-five and counting) but also as a place to hang out and even do business. The locus of all this congenial activity is a communal table that runs all the way from the front of the shop to the food case at the rear.

Crafted of four wide planks, the table is grooved down its center. It is surrounded by white, cup-like chairs that prove equally comfortable for elbows-on-the-table conversations, hunching over a laptop (WiFi access is free), or loafing with one of the newspapers or magazines displayed in the groove. A cushy banquette and a window seat offer more seating options for hanging out with friends.

One side of the shop is sheathed in barn siding, with inset shelves that display porcelain teaware by

Daisydog. Teapots, cookie jars, and cups and mugs in various sizes are decorated with snazzy circles (some are SubtleTea's logo)—five percent of proceeds go to PETA, the animal protection organization. The opposite wall showcases other tea-inspired products, such as soaps, soothing eye-teabags, bath teabags, and candles.

SubtleTeas are listed on a blackboard near the cash register—and a wall of jars whose leaves can be measured out by the ounce, too. Teas are categorized by the time of day, and there are also iced teas. There is tea latte and tea cappuccino, and a specialty of the shop is its bracing 'teaspresso.'

SubtleTea's menu spans breakfast and lunch with a variety of comestibles, such as sandwiches and salads and sweets, from vanilla and chocolate cupcakes to jumbo cookies.

sympathy for the kettle

109 Saint Mark's Place
bet. First Avenue and Avenue A
212-979-1650
www.sympathyforthekettle.com
Hours: Tuesday through Sunday 12 P.M. to
10 P.M.
Price Range: $

Formerly known as Michanna, Sympathy for the Kettle is snugly situated on Saint Mark's Place just a few steps west of Tompkins Square. New owner Jodi Holliday has repainted the narrow room a creamy raspberry, but otherwise the décor remains familiar to the tea spot's former habitués.

The diminutive space accommodates a mere five tables (plus a couple of sidewalk tables in warm weather), but it now boasts an inventory of over 150 teas, which are handsomely displayed in canisters along one wall. Each row is cast in a different pale metallic hue to signify a particular type of tea, be it black, green, decaffeinated, or herbal. The range includes plain and flavored blacks and greens, some rooibos and chais, and a series of South American mates. The tins are identified by luggage tags.

The blackboard hanging next to the serving counter lists the tearoom's menu of ready-to-pour "kettle" teas, which can be sipped on site or brewed to go. Especially popular are healing and detoxifying teas, which can be enhanced with a dash of ginger or ginseng. Savories and sweets are prepared daily, and they vary, depending upon the day. The red velvet cake, for example, arrives on Thursdays.

Sympathy for the Kettle goes beyond drinking tea; it also sells a small but discriminating array of tea things, both Western and Eastern in influence. Bodum's classic glass Chambor teapot is here, among others. Earl's Court drip catchers are available, too, as well as infusers. The tearoom will also make up gift baskets upon request.

t salon

AT THE CHELSEA MARKET

459 West 15th Street
bet. Ninth and Tenth Avenues
212-243-2259
www.tsalon.com
Hours: Daily 8 A.M. to 7:30 P.M.
Price Range: $

When the first edition of this book came out in 1995, its launch was celebrated at the first T Salon & T Emporium, which occupied premises under the old Guggenheim Museum in SoHo. Founder Miriam Novalle later moved her enterprise (and its Proper Afternoon Tea) to a brownstone in the Flatiron District. Now, she has set up shop at the Tenth Avenue end of the Chelsea Market in the Meatpacking District, downstream from Chelsea's art galleries.

This time out, Ms. Novalle has rejected languorous three-course teas in favor of speedy snacking and take-out tea. As she puts it, she is also now more "environmentally evolved." Designed by eco-savvy British architect Hans E. Knutsen and interior designer Lola Bodansky (with input from a feng shui master and a lighting designer), T Salon's interior is cloaked entirely in golden, sustainable bamboo. Two sinuous light fixtures created from translucent teabags by Swiss-born Eveline Feldman wind their way overhead. Countertops are made of concrete that has been tinted with tea. All products used and sold in the Salon, including packaging, cups, and napkins, are organic.

T Salon displays canisters containing 240 varieties and blends from Ms. Novalle's inventory of more than 400 teas. Samples can be sipped from tiny cast-iron teapots set up on warming stones before being measured out for purchase. Hot or iced tea can be taken away or consumed at a table at the back of the shop. Go-withs range from muffins and scones from Once Upon a Tart to more substantial fare, such as veggie-wraps. Two flat-screens list the teas available; alongside, a third screen is tuned to CNN, should you feel the need to catch up with the outside world.

tamarind tearoom

41–43 East 22nd Street
bet. Madison and Park Avenues
212-674-7400
www.tamarinde22.com
Hours: Daily 11:30 A.M. to 10 P.M.
Price Range: $$

Located next door to the serenely beautiful Indian restaurant of the same name, Tamarind Tearoom's hankie-sized space holds a mere five tables and a narrow counter for two. Teas—fourteen in all—are displayed in big square glass jars on shelves behind a backlit service bar, which also showcases a variety of sweets. Sets of vivid, psychedelic renderings of the gods Shiva and Natraj supply the only other decoration in the room. The mood here feels like a bracing cup of tea: soothing, yet snappy.

True to its indigenous cuisine, Tamarind offers a menu of delicious Indian sweets and sandwiches (as well as some British afternoon tea-style pastries for die-hard colonials). Indian desserts include Nan Khatai (soft, sweet cookies), Ajwani Sweet-and-Salt biscuits, and a traditional Indian relative of ice cream called Kulfi, which is made from solid frozen milk. Two light pastries—Ghujjia and Ghulab Jamnun—are filled, respectively, with semolina, raisins, coconut, and cashews; or dried milk and honey.

The selection of teas ranges over the map, from a Jasmine Pearl green to Nantou and Tiaguynyim oolongs and a white tea called Drum Mountain White Cloud. Two herbals feature herbs and floral scents of Hibiscus Elder, Violet, and Mint. There is also an herbal chai.

Tea can be ordered by the pot, but it is more relaxing to partake of Tamarind Tearoom's prix fixe, two-course tea, which is prepared for one person or two. The tea service includes a pot, a sandwich for each person (chosen from the list on the menu), and a "dessert sampler."

tavalon tea bar

22 East 14th Street
on Union Square West
bet. Fifth and University Avenues
212-807-7027
www.tavalon.com
Hours: Monday through Friday 8 A.M. to
10:30 P.M.; Saturday and Sunday 10 A.M. to
11:30 P.M.
Price Range: $

Even as they honor the history and mystique of tea, many purveyors (not only tea-leaf readers!) try to figure out what tea means today—and to project what it means for the future. Indeed, "the future of tea" is printed on the business cards of one of the newer and trendier tea spots in town: Tavalon Tea Bar. Tavalon is the brainchild of Jean-Paul Lee, a former management consultant, and Sonny Caberwal, an ex-attorney. Casting about for a way to avoid the corporate world, they decided to make tea their thing.

But how? By making the tea bar hip. Tavalon's teas are not blended; instead, they are "mixed," "unmixed," or "uncut." They are also mixed with a purpose: to boost energy or immunity, say, or to detox after a night on the town. One popular blend is Genius, a white tea with a hint of plum.

Designed by Anurag Nema (with Lee) as a silvery sliver, the tea bar is mirrored and tiled for a clean look. A DJ pumps out music from a tiny balcony, which projects over the serving counter. The pastry case features a selection of edibles from several downtown shops, such as 'wichcraft, Rice to Riches, Amai, and Balthazar Bakery. Tea-infused cookies are a special delight: try lemongrass and ginger, Earl Grey and currant, or green tea.

A sniffing station, with test tubes filled with samples of Tavalon's blends, was set up by tea sommelier Chris Cason as an educational and olfactory experience. Tavalon teas are also available in tins, which are displayed on shelves across from the skinny four-person counter. Although most customers drop in for a take-out tea, Tavalon does have one table for those who want to stay and sip.

tea & sympathy

108–110 Greenwich Avenue
bet. Seventh and Eighth Avenues
212-989-9735
www.teaandsympathynewyork.com
Hours: Monday through Friday 11:30 A.M. to
  10:30 P.M.; Saturday and Sunday 9:30 A.M. to
  10:30 P.M.
Price Range: $

If your average lovable British mum opened a tea-room, this might be it. With only eight oilcloth-draped tables, the miniscule space feels comfy but not crowded—even when it is, especially on weekends. Tea is properly brewed from leaves loose in the pot then strained into pretty teacups, not mugs. And it's perfectly all right to hold your teacup in one or both hands. No pinky-finger pretensions here.

To enhance the aura of insouciance and coziness, Tea & Sympathy's London Taxi—license plate "TANDS"—is usually parked regally out front. Inside the tearoom, apricot walls are hung with the mandatory portrait of H.R.H. Elizabeth II in full coronation regalia, a poster of cockney puns, and shelves displaying a miscellany of teapots, cups, saucers, and other teaware. Book-patterned wallpaper covers the divider separating the serving area from diners.

The menu speaks from the British heart and to the British tum: baked beans on toast, scotch eggs, treacle pudding, Bovril, and hot Ribena, a blackcurrant syrup much in favor across the pond. When British patrons descend, as they habitually do, they often request their toast with Marmite.

Tea & Sympathy offers two prix fixe tea menus. Cream Tea, composed of a pot of tea (choose from three dozen, from brands such as Typhoo and Yorkshire Gold) and scones with clotted cream and jam; and Afternoon Tea, with the traditional allotment of finger sandwiches (vegetarian ones, if desired), scones, and cake. You can also order tea by the pot, with or without a dessert.

Check out Tea & Sympathy's emporium next door. All sorts of Britstuff is available here, much of it blissfully irreverent. British tinned teas, they say, fly off the shelves.

the tea box

AT TAKASHIMAYA, NEW YORK

693 Fifth Avenue
bet. 54th and 55th Streets
212-350-0100
www.ny-takashimaya.com
Hours: Monday through Saturday 3 P.M. to
5 P.M.
Price Range: $$

Takashimaya is a sublime six-story repository of ultra-refined fashions for home and person, with a cross-cultural sensibility that embraces the best of Tokyo, Paris, and New York. To reach the Tea Box restaurant, which is on the lower level, you pass through Takashimaya's tea shop, an anteroom replete with Japanese tea things, including teapots, bowls, whisks, tea balls, and strainers (as well as biscuits and sweet jellies). The shop also offers a selection of teas packaged in bamboo boxes or tins, and several books that are classics in the field of tea and the tea ceremony.

Takashimaya's own blended loose-leaf teas are stored in silk-sheathed tea boxes in cubbies along the wall behind the counter. Samples are set out in bowls on the counter to assist you in making your selection. The array totals thirty-eight, including a rainbow of flavored and herbal teas, plus three rare specialties:

Assam Golden Tips, Ceylon Silvery Vintage, and a bright green matcha.

These same teas are on the menu for afternoon tea, which you can enjoy as a prix fixe repast or à la carte in either one of the Tea Box's two tearooms. Studies in the interplay of soft, neutral tones of sand and stone, both tearooms are tranquil sanctuaries clouded by billowing linen streamers across the ceiling. The rear room is somewhat quieter, set off by a partition.

The Tea Box's tea set offers a pot of tea accompanied by a sampler of sweet or savory delicacies and three cookies—either butter cookies by West and Yoki Motu or vegetable cookies by Suetomi. The East-West Afternoon Tea subscribes to the British prototype, with a "cross-cultural selection" of finger sandwiches, pastries, and cookies (instead of scones)—and fresh fruit.

The new Tea Garden on the top retail floor of Takashimaya, adorned with "pussy-willow" gates and accompanied by floral displays and a baby boutique, offers a tea set comprising seven exotic, healthful teas concocted from a variety of leaves, herbs, and fruit including mugwort, persimmon, and soybean. Desserts designed by chef Taro Mitsuiki incorporate green tea as a prime ingredient.

tea spot

127 MacDougal Street
bet. West 3rd Street and Washington
Square Park

212-505-0969

www.teaspotco.com

Hours: Monday through Saturday 10 A.M. to
10 P.M.; Sunday 10 A.M. to 8 P.M.

Price Range: $

Cheek-by-jowl with New York University and steps from Washington Square Park, Tea Spot offers a wide selection of teas in a long, narrow, library-like room dominated by a huge gridded shelf system displaying large tins of teas.

A brick wall runs behind the bar, separating tables that huddle at the front and at the rear of the tearoom. Because Tea Spot offers WiFi access with a $5 purchase, habitués often set up their laptops and settle in with papers and such, using the tearoom as an office-cum-study.

More, however, think of Tea Spot as a take-out joint, ambling up to the bar and ordering up a blend of teas that strike their fancy, or, in hotter weather, an iced tea latte—with or without 'pearls' to create a bubble tea—which will be "shaken or blended" to an individual's specifications.

Because tea is what counts, there are almost 100 to choose from. Helpful labels describe the contents of every canister; each is also color-coded to help identify the type of tea, be it black, green, white, a rooibos, a tisane, or a decaf. The names of the teas and their labels invite a quick read. Here's an excerpt for Tropical Cyclone: "Green Gencha and Assam with hibiscus, rose petals...mallow blossoms...passion fruit and pineapple." A small selection of tea pots, gift baskets and tea accessories fill a shelf near the front door, too.

teany

90 Rivington Street
bet. Orchard and Ludlow Streets
212-475-9190
www.teany.com
Hours: Sunday through Thursday 10 A.M. to
11 P.M.; Friday and Saturday 10 A.M. to
1 A.M.; cash only.
Price Range: $

Proprietors Moby and Kelly opened Teany as a vegetarian restaurant, but tea's the thing here. From its matcha-tinted walls to its ninety or so teas, teeny tiny Teany (with a dozen metal tables packed in the room and a couple more on the teenier terrace out front) proclaims a preference for this brew.

Teas are stored in canisters behind the serving counter and pastry shelf. Teany sells tea in two-ounce quantities, plus an array of paraphernalia including teapots, caddies, mugs, and tea balls. These are displayed along a second, skinnier counter near the front door.

A chubby metal notebook offers tea info from ingredients to caffeine counts. Teas are numbered and described: no. 24 Monkey Picked Superior Ti Kuan Yin is an oolong with an "orchid-like" flavor whose leaves and buds are, indeed, plucked by simian fingers; no. 98 Tea for the Liver is an antidote to a long night on the town; and no. 72 is "a sweet children's tea accented with blossoms, rosehip peels, and bits of apple."

Vegetarian tea sandwiches vary and typically include ploughman's cheddar and pickle, arugula and sundried tomato with white-bean spread, and avocado and cream (or tofu-cream) cheese. Along with regular scones, there is always a vegan scone of the day. A pair of sandwiches and a scone form Teany's Afternoon Tea Special, along with a pot and a choice of vegan petits fours.

ten ren's tea time

79 Mott Street
bet. Canal and Bayard Streets
212-732-7178 or 1-800-292-2049

www.tenrenusa.com

Hours: Sunday through Thursday 11 A.M. to
11 P.M.; Friday and Saturday 11 A.M. to 12 A.M.

Price Range: $

Taiwanese tea importers Ten Ren & Ginseng Company have operated a number of shops in the U.S. for more than thirty years, including three branches in the New York area—one in Manhattan on Mott Street; one in Queens on Roosevelt Avenue; and another in Brooklyn on Eighth Avenue. Two doors south on Mott is their most recent offshoot, Ten Ren's Tea Time (Ten Ren means "heavenly love"), a snappy bubble tea bar where you can sample the traditional black and green teas for which Ten Ren is justifiably renowned, as well as some of the trendiest tapioca teas in town. Ten Ren also offers by appointment what is known as a kung-fu tea; this is a highly specialized form of the tea ceremony concentrating on oolong teas, typically practiced exclusively by men.

The range of Ten Ren's teas is vast. Tapioca fruit teas are offered hot, iced, or warm, in 'regular' twelve-ounce or 'double' twenty-four-ounce portions. Fat, chewy tapioca pearls also enhance fruit, nut, bean, and green tea-flavored shredded ices and iced milk drinks, one of which blends coffee and tea for a particularly sweet and zesty buzz.

After your bubble tea, drop in at Ten Ren's elegant emporium up the street at 75 Mott Street. Here, owners Mark and Ellen Lii sell dozens of teas, some so fine they cost over $150 per pound. If you are uncertain about what to buy, there is a tasting table at the rear of the shop, where beautiful calligraphy and a wall painting set the mood—and where the Liis will help you make a selection. At the front of the shop, a 'family package' of green tea powder accompanied by a flyer extols the health benefits of green tea.

tracy stern's salontea

AT THE CITY CLUB HOTEL

55 West 44th Street
bet. Fifth and Sixth Avenues
212-398-1323
www.salontea.com
Hours: Tuesday through Saturday 2 P.M. to
6 P.M.; Sunday Noon to 3 P.M.
Price Range: $$$

Lifestyle entrepreneur Tracy Stern opened her first tea venture in Tampa, Florida, in 1994. An ardent traveler and art-history buff, she adjusted her focus when she moved to Manhattan. Inspired by seventeenth-century French salons, she now "holds court" at SalonTea at the hip City Club Hotel, which sits beside the Algonquin. Located on the hotel's mezzanine, SalonTea is a modernist haven decorated in an Hermès-inspired color scheme of orange and chocolate brown. Six tables for two ring a glass-protected oculus that overlooks the lobby below.

The prix fixe tea service begins with a presentation of SalonTea's six blended teas: The Artist, The Musician, The Writer, The Romantic, The Fashionable Dandy, and The Society Hostess. Ranging from black to green to rooibos, each is infused with its own hints of spice or flowers. Tea arrives with an egg timer so you can gauge the strength you desire; a warmer under the pot ensures the tea remains hot.

Scones in heart shapes are baked in Daniel Bouloud's DB restaurant on the ground floor. Inventive sandwiches include: petite corn muffins padded with egg salad and dill; cucumber rounds capped with alfalfa sprouts; and chicken salad studded with cranberry, walnut, raisin, apple, and pistachio. These are followed by chocolate cake to share topped with a chocolate frill, honey madeleines with edible lavender, and tea-infused truffles jetted in from Paris.

Tracy Stern also offers a range of BeauTea products and spa and catering services, and she hosts ChariTeas for local community organizations. Her book, Tea Party, written with Christie Matheson, features twenty menus for celebrations ranging from "fabulous showers to intimate gatherings."

Tracy Stern launched a Paris branch of SalonTea in 2007 at Franck et Fils, one of the city's most celebrated and fashionable department stores, on the Rue de Passy.

urasenke chanoyu center

153 East 69th Street
bet. Lexington and Third Avenues
212-988-6161
Call for schedule and to reserve.
Price Range: $$

The meditative Japanese tea ceremony known as Chanoyu elevates the making, serving, and drinking of tea to a high art. Toward the end of the sixteenth century, a revered tea master, Sen No Rikkyu, established the strict code of etiquette defining this ritual that continues to be practiced today. Chanoyu reflects four principles: harmony, respect, purity, and tranquility. These are sustained through every gesture during the ceremony.

In New York, you can experience an introduction to the Tea Ceremony at the Urasenke Chanoyu Center, which was established by a fifteenth-generation Grand Tea Master and President of the Urasenke Foundation of Kyoto, Dr. Shoshito Sen. Lectures and demonstrations are typically held once a month, on Wednesday evenings at 5:30 p.m.

Preparing to enter the tea room is a ritual in itself. After removing your shoes, you and other guests wait for a few minutes—an interval that affords you the opportunity to still your mind and shrug off the cares of the day. When the tea master arrives, you proceed into the tea room, empty except for tatami mats surrounding a small, square, sunken hearth. (For the lecture, tea is prepared outside the room.) At one end of the room, an elevated alcove exhibits a scroll brushed with calligraphy expressing the theme of the ceremony; a simple flower arrangement is meant to symbolize the fleeting beauty of nature. These are to be contemplated by the guests as they take their places.

The serving of the tea, a powdered green matcha, and an accompanying sweet, is a meditative experience, from the bow of thanks when offered the cup to the bows of thanks as the cup is passed from one guest to the next. A deep calm prevails—one, hopefully, that you will carry with you when you leave the center and re-enter the outside world.

and
some
more!

Who knew that taking tea in New York would turn up such a fascinating array of venues? Ten years ago, tea was just tea. Now it is a beverage, an ingredient in food, and a beauty product, among other things. There are so many places that serve tea, it was difficult to narrow the choice down to 50. Here are a dozen more that are worth a visit—and a cup or two…

bemelmans bar

AT THE CARLYLE HOTEL

35 East 76th Street
bet. Madison and Park Avenues
Entrance to the bar is on Madison Avenue
bet. 76th and 77th Streets
212-744-1600
www.thecarlyle.com
Hours: Weekends 1 P.M. to 4 P.M.
Price Range: $$$

One of the few tea venues around town dedicated to creating a delicious teatime experience for children is Bemelmans Bar, with its famed murals by the author/ illustrator of the beloved *Madeline* books. Prix fixe Madeline's Tea Parties are sensibly served at child-friendly hours on non-school days. Like adult teas in fine hotels, including the Carlyle's own Gallery (see page 48), the service is presented on a triple-tiered stand. China and linens are decorated with the Madeline imprint.

Special treats include a scrumptious sundae topped with a bright red cherry. Copies of the *Madeline* books are at hand to browse, and there's a pianist who will take requests for favorite songs. "Thank Heaven for Little Girls," anyone? Finally: little girls who can legally claim the name Madeline—via a school ID or passport—will be treated to a free tea when accompanied by an adult.

fitzers

AT THE FITZPATRICK HOTEL

687 Lexington Avenue
bet. 56th and 57th Streets
212-784-2570
www.fitzpatrickhotels.com
Hours: Daily 3 P.M. to 6 P.M.
Price Range: $$

A quiet enclave of Gaelic charm secreted in a small hotel steps away from the bustle of two of Manhattan's brightest Blooms—Bloomingdale's and Bloomberg—Fitzers is the New York outpost of an Irish family-owned hotel chain. The cozy restaurant, carpeted appropriately in mossy Gaelic green, is laid out in an inviting manner with two tables snugly situated in front of a fireplace, and others in cubbies at the rear of the L-shaped room: perfect for private tête-à-têtes, be they business deals or deals of another, more tantalizingly indiscreet persuasion.

The teas here, as they rightly should be, are imported from Ireland, from Barry's, and include a regular or decaf black blend, Earl Grey, and a green tea, plus chamomile and peppermint. The prix fixe menu is similar for both Fitzers Low Tea and Fitzers High Tea, the only difference being that the Low version offers either finger sandwiches or scones and cookies while the High Tea includes all three.

forty carats

AT BLOOMINGDALE'S

Lexington Avenue
bet. 59th and 60th Streets
212-705-2000
www.bloomingdales.com
Hours: Daily 10 A.M. to 7 P.M.
Price Range: $$

Best known for its frozen yogurts and smoothies, Forty Carats has opened a bright, modernistic café on the sixth floor of the venerable department store Bloomingdale's, just behind the bedlinens department.

Teas—both hot and cold—come courtesy of Tavalon (see page 104), and are defined both by the blend of tealeaves and other infusions and how they will affect your mood. Thus, the menu obliges with the following: calming, antiaging, energizing, slimming, and balancing. The latter suffuses a detox black with peppermint and ginger.

Although the overall range of foods offered at Forty Carats runs the gamut from salads to sandwiches to the aforementioned smoothies, mid-afternoon blahs are typically remedied with sweets such as pound cake, brownies, blondies, or a tasty treat known as a "sweet bar."

During the summer months, Tavalon is also responsible for Forty Carats's chai iced teashakes.

goodman's

AT BERGDORF GOODMAN

745 Fifth Avenue
bet. 58th and 59th Streets
212-753-7300
www.bergdorfgoodman.com
Hours: Monday through Friday 2:30 P.M. to 6 P.M.
Price Range: $$

Goodman's, one of Bergdorf's two restaurants (the other is BG on the seventh floor, see page 30), is located down a short flight of stairs at the northeast corner of the bustling lower-level Beauty Floor. After running the gauntlet through atomizers spritzed by a phalanx of chattering salespeople, it is a great relief to be led to a banquette for a restorative cup of tea—or a more substantial repast.

The room is anchored by a long central table. Two walls are sheathed in celadon grasscloth; the third is painted a soothing, softly-lit aqua, which serves as a backdrop for a huge looking-glass. Banquettes along the two long walls are upholstered in snappy stripes, and chairs, creamy white, are padded at back and seat. No need for fancy napery here; tables are topped with ivory-toned plastic laminate.

Most of the teas hail from Harney & Sons; for a brisk pick-me-up, there's a hearty Lipton orange pekoe as well. The galaxy of sweets is delicious, and changes intermittently: tea and desserts may be ordered prix fixe or à la carte.

gramstand

214 Avenue A
bet. 13th and 14th Streets
212-533-1934
www.gramstand.com
Hours: Monday through Friday 7 A.M. "until
    rather late;" weekends 9 A.M., ditto
Price range: $

With its free WiFi, Gramstand functions more as a student center-cum-writing retreat than as a bonafide tea room. With power strips galore, everyone is seemingly plugged in—both upstairs and down—in a cozy cave of a lounge. Obviously in the East Village a downtown sensibility prevails, so the décor is casual, with metallic-hued walls lined with art (for sale), comfy-schlumpy couches, a sprinkling of tables, and chairs of varying shapes to accommodate singles or groups—as well as several strands of Christmas lights. To prime the creative pump, Gramstand offers short-lists of specially blended teas in two major categories: ancient (a.k.a. estate teas) and modern. The latter are styled as "concoctions . . . orchestrated with gourmet herbs and ingredients." The traditional tea line-up comprises a single white, a green, a black, an oolong, an Earl Gray, and a Kyoto Roast. There is also a nice sensory spectrum of fruit teas and wellness teas, such as a Dragon Honey Mint, as well as latte teas, including a Velvet Vanilla Teaccucino. The menu of go-withs is succinct: a muffin of the day and croissants, as well as an assortment of brownies, cupcakes, and homemade granola bars. There is also a daily special sandwich and quiche.

The place, we overheard, "gets wild at night"; on Thursdays, Gramstand dedicates two hours—7 P.M. to 9 P.M.—to live jazz.

housing works
used books and café

126 Crosby Street
bet. Prince and Houston Streets
212-334-3324
www.housingworks.org
Hours: Monday through Friday 10 A.M. to
9 P.M.; Saturday and Sunday Noon to 7 P.M.
Price Range: $

Since 1990, Housing Works, New York's largest AIDS

organization, has opened a number of thrift shops whose proceeds go to providing housing and job training for men and women with HIV and AIDS—more than 15,000 so far.

Some time ago, Housing Works took over an existing used-book store in a big, old-fashioned double-height loft space on Crosby Street. The vast selection of books is collected in well-marked bays along the walls, as well as on a balcony and on tables throughout the store. (A $50 membership in Housing Works is an outreach effort to help fight AIDS, "one book at a time.")

The cafe at the back of the store offers eight bagged teas from +AZO, plus Bigelow's English Breakfast and a Celestial Seasonings herbal. Teas are poured in three sizes—to stay or go. Baked goodies are prepared by Eli's and include muffins, brownies, and fruit-crumble bars.

king's carriage house

251 East 82nd Street
bet. Second and Third Avenues
212-734-5490
www.kingscarriagehouse.com
Hours: Daily 3 P.M. to 4 P.M.; reservations
   required.
Price Range: $$

When Elizabeth King met her future husband, Paul Farrell, in his native Ireland, she confessed to him that she'd love to replicate Irish manor-house hospitality in New York. Some time ago, the couple realized their dream, converting a former bookshop in a charming, Upper East Side carriage house into a homey place to lunch, dine—or take tea.

King's Carriage House's prix fixe, traditional afternoon tea is served under the languid gaze of three antlered stags in the sunny yellow Willow Room, which looks out into a tiny slip of garden. Irish-blend leaf tea accompanies cucumber-topped triangles of crustless bread, salmon on toast, and curried chicken tartlets, plus mini scones with jam and an array of sweets.

The front room of the building is given over to the sale of teaware. Upstairs, the Red and Hunt Rooms—seating twenty-eight and sixteen respectively—are available for private teas.

kitchenette

1272 Amsterdam Avenue
bet. 122nd and 123rd Streets
212-531-7600
Hours: Monday through Friday 8 A.M. to 11 P.M.;
   Saturday and Sunday 9 A.M. to 11 P.M.
Price Range: $

"Comfort food at its best" and "food reminiscent of childhood memories" were the goals—the mantras, really—of friends and colleagues Lisa Hall and Ann Nickinson when they began their culinary collaboration some fifteen years ago. The Kitchenette on Amsterdam (there is also a downtown outpost at 156 Chambers Street) is the kind of eatery that promises ample blue-plate, home-cooked meals in a relaxed, homespun environment that seduces through deliciousness, both of plate and place.

The decor at Kitchenette is shamelessly retro. Fans twirl lazily from the tin ceiling and fanciful metal flowers sprout from lawn-green wainscoting. Tables, flanked by no-nonsense chairs covered in red leatherette, are topped with chicken-mesh glass, a pattern echoed on the tile floor. A blackboard announces the daily specials.

During the afternoon, when the place quiets down, Kitchenette is the perfect spot to hang out with a mug of tea and one of their yummy home-baked desserts—or a homemade buttermilk biscuit or scone, this being afternoon "breakfast" after all.

the lobby

AT THE ALGONQUIN HOTEL

59 West 44th Street
bet. Fifth and Sixth Avenues
212-840-6800
www.algonquinhotel.com
Hours: Daily 11:30 A.M. to 10:45 P.M.
Price Range: $

To partake of tea at the Algonquin, or "Gonk," is to sample something of American literary and theatrical history. The hotel opened its doors in 1902, attracting personalities such as Douglas Fairbanks, Sr., Gertrude Stein, and Eudora Welty. After World War I, Dorothy Parker, Robert Benchley, and other writers and critics—most of them associated with *The New Yorker* just around the corner—started their famed Round Table in the hotel's Oak Room.

Although, alas, the hotel does not offer a traditional afternoon tea as such, it is well worth a visit for its sense of place—and a simple pot of tea. The Gonk's refurbished lobby has lost none of its charm; its genial mélange of squashy velvet sofas, wingchairs, and armchairs still invokes a "gentleman's club" atmosphere of lazy indulgence. Reading lights abound, so, if you are in the neighborhood and are so inclined, stop in, order a tea, and wile away an hour or so with a newspaper. No one will disturb you.

sarabeth's

ON AMSTERDAM AVENUE

423 Amsterdam Avenue
bet. 80th and 81st Streets
212-496-6280
www.sarabeths.com
Hours: Monday through Friday 3:30 P.M. to
   5:30 P.M.
Price Range: $$

A mainstay on Amsterdam Avenue two blocks west of the American Museum of Natural History, the West Side Sarabeth's is a country-cozy sort of spot where taking tea, either alone or with a companion, seems as natural and friendly as snuggling up with a cuppa at home.

At teatime, one table is "propped" for tea, so you can inspect the edible line-up before you order. The top level of the tiered stand displays tea sandwiches, such as chicken salad dotted with apples, raisins, walnuts, and dill; the second features mini scones with whipped cream and one of Sarabeth's signature jams; the bottom presents an assortment of cookies, including a chocolate chip one that's almost as big as a saucer. Tea arrives in a colorful, chubby pot and hot water can be refreshed upon request; you can also add a glass of bubbly champagne or Lillet.

sarabeth's

ON CENTRAL PARK SOUTH

40 Central Park South
bet. Fifth and Sixth Avenues

212-826-5959

www.sarabeths.com

Hours: Monday through Friday 3:30 P.M. to
5 P.M.; Saturday and Sunday 4 P.M. to 5 P.M.

Price Range: $$

On Central Park South, a snappy Sarabeth's occupies the premises of Rumpelmeyer's, a former beloved emporium of confectionary indulgence. The location is just across the avenue from a line-up of horses and carriages, should you wish to precede your afternoon tea with a gentle lope around the pond at the southern end of the park.

The front room contains the bar; here, too, is where to enjoy a delicious, full-course tea, relaxing on a banquette padded with faux zebra skin, or on comfy bistro chairs pulled up to a table roomy enough for edibles—and later, drinks?

tea & tea

51 Mott Street
bet. Bayard and Pell Streets
212-393-9009
Hours: Daily 11 A.M. to 11:30 P.M.
Price Range: $

Bubble tea bars literally "bubble" along the heavily trafficked stretch of Mott Street between Canal Street and the courthouses just north of City Hall. Tea & Tea is a standout from the norm, with walls painted metallic silver and vibrant gunpowder tea green.

Tea & Tea prides itself on its wide variety of tea drinks, including a round-up of fruit-infused green teas. They also have a number of what they term "exotic drinks;" three of these—Passionate Temptation, Verdant Cooler, and Crimson Sensation—are also made more refreshing with green tea infusions.

As in many Chinese restaurants, you make your Tea & Tea selection by number. Passionate Temptation, for example, is no. 73, while plain black tea is no. 19. Three Chinese teas—ginseng oolong, honey ginseng, and Dragon Pearl Jasmine—are only served hot. House recommendations are bulleted, as are some of the snacks, which run the gamut from toast slathered with condiments such as condensed milk, coconut butter, or peanut butter, to green tea cheesecake, jumbo tea eggs, mango, and sesame pudding.

glossary
and
index

varieties of tea

Tea connoisseurs cite over 3,000 varieties of tea, each with its own distinct character. As with fine wine, the quality of the tea is determined by climate, soil, and weather conditions, as well as by the expertise of the tea grower. Altitude makes a difference; some highly esteemed tea estates cling to the sides of mountains, making access to the shrubs difficult and the plucking of the leaves an arduous endeavor. Courage and labor only add to the mystique surrounding some rare premium teas.

Almost ninety-five percent of all tea produced ends up in tea bags. The rest comprises prime-quality leaves and buds, often grown organically, which are plucked by machine or by hand for premium teas. What distinguishes one tea from another is the process of its manufacture after plucking. This process is composed of several steps: drying the leaves to rid them of moisture; rolling the leaves to release oils and enzymes; oxidizing (or fermenting) them; and finally, drying them once again. Variations in the process result in differing intensities of hue: black, green, oolong, and white.

Tea may grow in the wild, but most are cultivated on plantations or on small estates known as tea gardens. Darjeelings are Indian teas that often bear the name of the tea garden where they were produced; they can be further defined by the timing of their harvest, or flush. The first flush occurs in early spring, resulting in a delicate tea; teas from the second or later flushes have more body.

WHITE teas are the most delicate, whose leaves are harvested in early spring. Tightly furled, the balled-up leaves reveal a silvery cast. Leaves are withered for several hours, a process that causes them to lose almost half their original moisture-weight through evaporation, and are then lightly roasted to remove all but ten percent of the remaining moisture and to seal in their delicate flavor. Whites undergo no oxidation; they are not fermented.

GREEN teas are not oxidized either. After leaves and buds are plucked, they are usually spread out on trays made of bamboo and left to dry until most of the moisture has evaporated. The leaves are then swiftly heated to halt oxidation and prevent fermentation. Often the leaves are twisted or rolled to assume singular shapes, such as pellets. As the tea steeps in the cup, the leaves gently unfurl.

OOLONG leaves are partially withered, shaken to release enzymes, and fermented as long as necessary to create a particular tea. Short fermentation results in a green-tea-like tea; longer fermentations impart honey-like or amber tones.

BLACK teas undergo the lengthiest process. After plucking, leaves are withered, then rolled and re-rolled several times to release oils and enzymes, after which they are fully oxidized, then fired. The firing halts oxidation at the precise moment required to lend character to a specific tea. These days, leaves are shredded by a machine (called a CTC because it Crushes, Tears, and Curls the leaves), which cuts fermentation time in half during the withering process. CTC-assisted commercial-grade teas generally have a uniform appearance and taste.

PU-ERH tea leaves are not oxidized, but they are fermented, and aged in caves for many years; the dampness in the caves lends them their distinctive earthy flavor. Pu-erhs are often molded into shapes, such as bricks or rounds.

FLAVORED teas receive their particular flavorings during the fermentation cycle; flavorings enhance a black- or green-based tea by imparting a particular "note" such as jasmine, ginger, or rose. Some tea makers combine different flavors.

HERBAL TEAS, also known as tisanes or infusions, are not really teas at all, but are grouped in the same "family" of beverages because they are brewed in the same manner. Composed of leaves and/or flowers, tisanes are taken to aid digestion or to soothe the spirit; a number are believed to manifest other medicinal properties as well.

ROOIBOS, sometimes called "red teas" because of the reddish cast of their leaves, are herbals grown in South Africa. Rich in antioxidants and high in vitamin C, these herbal teas have long been appreciated for their perceived medicinal value. Because they contain very little tannin, prolonged steeping will not cause a rooibos to taste bitter; in fact, some benefit from an extended steeping time—up to twenty minutes, or more. Rooibos teas can also be reheated.

storing tea

When you purchase loose-leaf tea by the ounce, transfer it as soon as possible to an opaque container such as an airtight tin and store it in a cupboard, away from light and heat. If you do so, your tea should stay fresh for months. Tea fades when exposed to light, so a glass container is inadvisable. Tea is also adversely affected by moisture, so it should not be refrigerated or frozen. Tea bags should also be kept in a cool, dry location, away from light; if you transfer them from the box in which they were purchased, do store them in a similar manner as loose-leaf tea.

how to make a cup of black tea

Fill a kitchen kettle with cold water. (Cold water contains more oxygen than hot water; it is the oxygen that creates bubbles in the water, which cause furled tea leaves to open and release their flavor.)

Bring water to a rolling boil. Do not overboil or underboil. Overboiling causes water to lose oxygen, which will cause the tea to taste muddy. Underboiling results in a thin, tasteless, tepid tea.

While the water is coming to a boil, run hot water from the tap into the teapot. Let the hot water sit in the teapot for two or three minutes, swirl, and pour out.

Measure tea leaves into the teapot—one heaping teaspoon per cup. The warmth of the teapot will allow the dry tea leaves to begin to relax in anticipation of their immersion in the boiling water.

Bring the teapot to the kettle—not vice versa! Every moment counts when preparing a proper cup of tea!

Pour boiling water over the tea leaves in the teapot. The leaves will double in size as they steep. Let the tea steep for three to five minutes. (Brewing times vary, so consult your tea tin for the optimum time. Over-brewing will make the tea taste bitter.) Stir the tea gently before pouring.

Pour a small amount of tea through a strainer into a teacup. Dilute to taste with hot water from the kettle. Add milk, if desired—or lemon. (Many tea drinkers opt to pour milk into the cup first; this practice came into being to ensure that a fragile porcelain cup not break when boiling water was poured into it. These days, most teacups can withstand the heat, especially if they are dishwasher-proof.)

Black teas turn bitter after sitting in the teapot too long and should be replenished. Other teas, such as oolongs, maintain their flavor through multiple infusions.

Rinse the teapot after use; do not wash with soap as this leaves a residue that affects the taste of subsequent pours.

how to make a cup of green tea

Bring warm water just barely to the boiling point; the water should be piping hot, but not actually bubbling. Green tea leaves are very delicate and the action of bursting bubbles is too violent for them. Boiling water also causes green teas to taste bitter.

Rinse the teapot with hot water, pour it into a kettle, then place a teaspoon or two of tea leaves into the warmed teapot.

Let water in the kettle sit for two or three minutes to cool slightly, then pour over the tea leaves in the teapot. Steep a minute or so, strain, and pour tea into a teacup.

Many green teas can be steeped at least three times before discarding the leaves. In fact, the Chinese believe that subsequent infusions—up to seven—bring increasing amounts of good luck.

index by neighborhood